BOXING THE KANGAROO

A Reporter's Memoir

BOXING THE KANGAROO

A Reporter's Memoir

Robert J. Donovan

University of Missouri Press
Columbia and London

Copyright © 2000 by
The Curators of the University of Missouri
University of Missouri Press, Columbia, Missouri 65201
Printed and bound in the United States of America
All rights reserved
5 4 3 2 1   04 03 02 01 00

Library of Congress Cataloging-in-Publication Data

Donovan, Robert J.
    Boxing the kangaroo: a reporter's memoir / Robert J. Donovan.
        p. cm.
    Includes index.
    ISBN 0-8262-1281-6 (alk. paper)
    1. Donovan, Robert J. 2. Journalists—United States—Biography. I. Title.

PN4874.D685 A3 2000
070'.92—dc21
[B]   00-028626

∞™ This paper meets the requirements of the
American National Standard for Permanence of Paper
for Printed Library Materials, Z39.48, 1984.

Design and composition: Vickie Kersey DuBois
Printer and binder: Thomson-Shore, Inc.
Typefaces: Minion, Rockwell

*Frontispiece drawing by Ray Driver, courtesy
University of Maryland College of Journalism*

In Memory of Four Editors Who Made a Difference in My Life:

Evan W. Thomas, Sr.
Edward Kuhn, Jr.
Nick B. Williams
L. L. Engelking

Contents

Preface   ix

1. Breaking In on Seven Dollars a Week until the Pay Cut Came   1
2. My Friend Fiorello   8
3. How a Replacement Got into Combat   13
4. Getting to Know Washington and Franklin D. Roosevelt's
   Proper Choice   29
5. A Phenomenon   38
6. Wake Island—and Beyond   41
7. Harry Truman's Hearty Departure   47
8. Inside Story   50
9. Who Said John Foster Dulles Couldn't Tell a Fib?   55
10. A Newspaper Reporter Swamped in Classified Documents   59
11. A "Most Unorthodox" Best-Seller   62
12. No Other Stag Dinner Like It   68
13. Chief of the *New York Herald Tribune* Washington Bureau   70
14. Twentieth-Century Odyssey: President Eisenhower's
    Megatrip to Asia and India   75
15. Things I Learned under the Capitol Dome   83
16. Score One for Jock Whitney   92
17. Chronicling John Kennedy's Close Calls on *PT 109* and *PT 59* 95
18. Chief of the *Los Angeles Times* Washington Bureau   110
19. "Where Is the President Anyway?"   113
20. Travels with Lyndon   123
21. The Big Story That Fell in My Lap   128
22. A Roundabout Way to the Good Years   130
23. What Next?   134

Index   137

PREFACE

In a long career as a reporter in Buffalo, New York City, Paris, and Washington, and as the author of ten published books, including *PT 109: John F. Kennedy in World War II* and a two-volume history of the Truman presidency, I experienced unexpected and sometimes astonishing events, and at least one that was unspeakably sorrowful.

For several years I was chief of the *New York Herald Tribune* Washington bureau. Later, I was for several years chief of the *Los Angeles Times* Washington bureau.

Mayor Fiorello H. La Guardia of New York sent blood flowing from my cheek when he angrily slammed the door of his car on me. Then, in the most unlikely event of my life, he inquired whether I would like to be secretary of the New York City Fire Department.

On Plum Pudding Island in the South Pacific, in 1961, while retracing the steps of former Lieutenant Kennedy as skipper of *PT 109* in 1943, I picked up a stick of coral as a souvenir for him. In 1995, after his death, it was sold at an auction in New York (not by me) for $68,500.

At an outing on a ranch in Australia, President Lyndon B. Johnson pressed me into boxing a kangaroo and then cheered on the kangaroo.

Mindlessly, in the war in Europe, I almost walked into the German lines while taking cigarettes to a friend who manned a machine gun in one of our forward positions.

Once President Truman became angry at the wrong man: me.

Ironically, in view of things to come, in 1959 I incurred the unjustified suspicion of Vice President Richard M. Nixon that I had secretly taped his conversation.

Through firsthand observation I learned the potential danger of ordering bean soup in the Senate dining room in the Capitol.

In the fall of 1955, to enable me to write the story of Dwight D. Eisenhower's first three years as president, top-secret documents were brought to me daily in loaded carts in an office assigned to me in the White House. Legally, I was permitted to read the documents because the White House got me a highly rated Q-clearance, yet a congressional investigation was threatened. Eisenhower was not even aware of my presence. However, the book for which I was researching became number one on the *New York Times* best-sellers list for fourteen weeks.

In a single trip abroad in 1959, covering Eisenhower, I saw, among other places, the Vatican, the Appian Way, the Colosseum, the Parthenon, the

Khyber Pass, the Taj Mahal, the Tomb of Kemel Atatürk in Turkey, the Tomb of Mohammad Ali Jinnah in Pakistan, the Arc de Triomphe, the Louvre, and the Prado in Madrid.

I was in a press bus behind President Kennedy when his motorcade turned in front of the Texas School Book Depository in Dallas, the equivalent of Ford's Theatre in Washington on April 14, 1865.

In 1948, I heard President Truman give 'em hell at every whistle-stop in the land.

It was not the career I had intended, nor the life I might have expected. The happenstance of graduating from high school at the peak of the Great Depression diverted me from Yale University to the post of copyboy on the *Buffalo Courier Express*. In retrospect, I wouldn't have had it any other way.

BOXING THE KANGAROO

A Reporter's Memoir

1

Breaking In on Seven Dollars a Week until the Pay Cut Came

In the 1920s in Buffalo, New York, my father, Michael J. Donovan—a lovable man whose own schooling ended with the seventh grade in his native coal-mining town of Morris Run, Pennsylvania—was proud that he was planning to send me to Hotchkiss in preparation for Yale. It was only a matter of time, however, before the Great Depression crushed his highly successful career as an interior decorator and property owner. My own formal education ended in the gloom of 1932 when I graduated from Lafayette High School, a good public school in our neighborhood.

As fear spread, people worried about their own resources and stopped spending money on, for example, new interior decoration for their houses. My father owned perhaps a dozen houses in upper-class neighborhoods. As was his disposition, he decorated each of them in expectation of sizable profits, but in the financial climate sales vanished. He owned outright or in partnership one of the best medical buildings in the city, on Delaware Avenue. Suddenly doctors and dentists could not collect on their bills and fell behind in paying their rent. My father lost his investment in the building. He became all the more depressed because he blamed himself for his predicament. He resigned from his two country clubs and from the Buffalo Club, the elite men's club in the city, the former presidents of which had included Millard Fillmore and Grover Cleveland. Now he was stripped of his two favorite pastimes, golf and pre-luncheon pool games. He drove his Packard less. One gratification was the excited welcome home he received each evening from his beloved wirehaired terrier named Chap. Chap took the Depression in stride but was a nervous wreck over everything else. He once chewed away part of a sleeve of a tuxedo my father had bought during a trip to Italy in 1923.

My father was chagrined that the allowance he gave me every week practically dwindled away. Already Hotchkiss and Yale were memories. The first time I was to be in a college classroom would be fifty-two years later as Ferris Professor of Journalism at Princeton.

In the Depression one of the responsibilities undertaken by public school principals was helping to find jobs for students who were graduating without any hope of going to college. When I went to the Lafayette principal, Captain (retired) Calvert K. Mellen, in search of help, he inquired what kind of business I wanted to get into. My best marks at Lafayette were in English composition. And with Governor Franklin D. Roosevelt preparing to run for president and Adolf Hitler's shadow falling across Germany, I followed news avidly. An older cousin noticed this, and she said I ought to become a newspaper reporter.

I mentioned this to Cap Mellen, as we called him. On my behalf he telephoned a friend, Fred McLennan, managing editor of the *Buffalo Courier-Express*, the morning newspaper. Shortly I found myself in McLennan's office. A taciturn man, he said he could give me a job as a night copyboy for the summer while the regulars were on vacation. I began in July 1933, at a salary of seven dollars a week; my hours were from 6:00 to 11:00 six nights a week. I was thrilled to be working for a newspaper and determined to be the best copyboy the *Courier-Express* ever had. My eagerness exasperated editors, but the problems did not end there. I plowed into Walter Lippmann's books on journalism without making allowances that some of his theories did not apply at my level.

One of my duties, shortly before the press run each night, was to pick up photo cuts in the photo-engraving room, take them to Joe Myers, the pugnacious foreman of the composing room, and then, after he had made certain notations on a chart, deliver them to the stereotype department. One of these rounds occurred on the same day I had read a passage in Lippmann criticizing the practice of channeling news through third persons. This made perfect sense to me, so instead of taking that day's cuts to Myers and then to the stereotype department, I went straight to stereotyping, proud of my minor contribution to the efficiency of the paper.

I was probably still complimenting myself in the newsroom when the door from the composing room burst open. With his sleeves rolled up, the red-faced Myers charged at me as though he was coming out of his corner in a boxing ring. "Where the hell are those cuts?" he yelled. "The edition is being held up." As he seemed to be reaching for my throat, I managed to tell him I had delivered them to stereotyping. Of course, he never would have looked for them there since he first had to check them. In Washington years later, I recounted the episode over lunch to Lippmann, thinking he would be amused. He wasn't.

At least Myers didn't threaten to have me fired. Those threats came soon enough from some of the older reporters, especially from one short-tempered woman among them. On the far wall of the newsroom was a line of telephone booths where reporters could make or receive calls. I was responsible for answering incoming calls. I didn't, and the reporters grew increasingly indignant. The reason I did not answer the phones was that I did not hear them ringing. I was so alarmed by threats to have me fired that I went to a specialist. His tests indicated that it was difficult for me to hear "high dropping-off notes," such as distant ringing telephones. An older cousin of mine was an officer in the National Guard and what we might call today a "gun nut." He had set up a firing range in our basement. Like most houses in Buffalo, ours was heated by coal. Our target was safely in the coal bin, which we could fire into from the open part of the basement. By my early years in high school, I was consistently hitting the bull's-eye with a .45-caliber Colt automatic pistol. When we were finished for the day my right ear rang painfully. Some nerves were impaired, but not so seriously as to keep me out of the infantry when war came.

When the vacation season at the *Courier-Express* ended in 1932, the managing editor called me in, I supposed, to tell me that he had to let me go because the regular copyboys had returned. Not at all. He said I could go on working three nights a week, but he would have to cut my weekly pay to $6.30. I was at once grateful and determined that my future should lie elsewhere, even though in stages I became a reporter earning $13.00 a week.

My first assignment, fortunately brief, was the day police beat. Late one afternoon, the police announced that a minor gang member had been shot and killed. Our files had no photograph of him. We got his address through the police, and a photographer and I were sent to his shabby house to borrow a picture of the victim, or at least take a photograph of one. A tough-looking man answered the doorbell. Our request made him downright menacing. The photographer pulled me back down the stairs and said he knew another way to get a photo.

We drove to the county morgue, where the photographer was obviously well known to the attendants. After he explained his problem, one of the men led us into the hideous, acid-smelling environment of what I shall call, for lack of knowledge, the refrigeration room. The attendant checked names in a docket, then led the photographer to a numbered drawer in a stark white wall. They opened it and pulled out a slab on which the victim lay, his body wrapped in a sheet. The dead man was of slight build, so the two of them had no difficulty lifting the corpse to an upright position on an autopsy table. Ignoring the closed eyes, the photographer took a couple of facial shots. I watched from the farthest corner of the room but could see no wound. Back at the paper the "artist" painted opened eyes on the film. Readers of the paper the next morning saw a front-page photograph of a man with an unmistakably cadaverous look.

I remember vividly another episode I witnessed at the *Courier-Express*. The foreign editor, the sole person handling foreign news, worked from a single desk adjoining the large circular night copy desk. He was a slender, somewhat fussy, middle-aged man with what I remember as a slight English accent. I never heard any complaints about his competence. He worked alone very seriously. Copy brought from the wire service printers was perpetually piled in a sprawl.

One night there was a stir in the place. A former and obviously popular reporter who had left before my time came off the elevator. As he walked through the newsroom, a definite merriment spread, as if we were in the presence of a prankster. When he reached the foreign desk, the editor characteristically tried to pay no attention to nonsense. The visitor, who was probably a bit tipsy, reached into his overcoat pocket and pulled out a garter snake, which I saw distinctly. Without a word, he tossed it onto the pile of copy on the editor's desk. As the startled editor scrambled from his chair, the snake wriggled out of sight among the papers. And that was all there was to the shocker. The snake slithered to the floor and disappeared behind a radiator set in the wall, under a window. To my knowledge, no one ever saw it again. The next day, I forgot to check on how much foreign news had made it into the paper.

On reflection, why should any of us have been concerned about a garter snake? No receptionist was stationed at the entrance to the newsroom. Anyone could walk in from the sidewalk, take the elevator to our floor, and approach the city editor in quest of publicity for his wares. One afternoon, a huckster came in with a huge carton and hoisted it onto an empty desk. Trying to interest an editor in a story, the man opened the box to display a boa constrictor. Mercifully, it was in a stupor. The man and his monster were soon back on the sidewalk. No story.

Occasionally, if I was not covering crimes or outings of the Odd Fellows or the Elks, I was tackling lofty suggestions sent down by the advertising or circulation departments. To please advertising I would be assigned to write about a building boom in Buffalo, the residents of which in the early thirties were so broke they could scarcely put up kennels. Circulation liked to see stories about the magnificent, cool summer climate in Buffalo, reminding readers how foolish it would be to head for the mountains or the seashore instead of staying home and enjoying the *Courier-Express* in breezes from Canada.

At least three years and a modest amount spent on railroad fares from Buffalo were what it took me to get a job as a reporter on the *New York Herald Tribune* in December 1937. It was worth that and much more. I had been writing futilely to the *Herald Tribune* and the *New York Times*. One scant reply from the *Times* declared that in the Depression the paper was getting so many applications for jobs that, were they all placed side by side, they would stretch from Times Square to the George Washington Bridge spanning the Hudson River.

Inevitably, this refocused my quest on the *Herald Tribune*. It was not the only reason, however. In my reading of the two newspapers, I found more liveliness in, and took more pleasure from, the *Herald Tribune*. Walter Lippmann's columns there were compelling. I feasted on Stanley Woodward's stories of the big college football games. (Red Smith came later.) Doubtless, there were explanations unknown to me, but sometimes the play of news in the *Times* seemed peculiar. On its front page on January 31, 1933, for example, the lead story was datelined Albany, N.Y., and began:

> New or additional taxes of an aggregate of $84,000,000 were recommended by Governor Lehman in his annual budget message, which was transmitted to the Legislature this evening with his constitutional budget bill, calling for total appropriations for the next fiscal year from all funds and for all purposes of $234,998,531, a decrease of $23.7 million.

On the same front page that January 31, the paper off-led with (that is, placed in the column at the extreme left side of the page, a treatment denoting secondary importance or interest) a story from Berlin, which began:

> Adolf Hitler, leader of the National Socialist party, today was appointed Chancellor of Germany after being twice rejected last year for that office.

For the *New York Times* to give secondary play to news of Hitler's strengthened grip on power seemed incredible.

Charles McLendon, a Texan, was city editor of the *Herald Tribune* when I was working full-time as a reporter in Buffalo and craving to get to New York. A letter to him would do me no good. A hometown friend of mine whose father worked on the *Herald Tribune* told me that the Reid family, which owned the paper, also had ties with Yale and pressed the city desk to hire "Yale boys." I was never to see evidence of this, even though, to be sure, Yale was represented in the newsroom. Anyhow, the thought of "Yale boys" wasn't a pleasant one for me in the mid-1930s.

Early in 1935, I climbed into an upper berth on an overnight train to New York. The next afternoon, I arrived at the *Herald Tribune* and, of course, encountered the elderly receptionist for the editorial department. Since I did not have an appointment, she had the authority, so to speak, to send me back to Buffalo empty-handed. She inquired why I wanted to see the city editor. I told her. Her reply admonished me that I was taking the wrong path. I would have to begin by writing a letter and filling out an application for the job. "But this is my day off," I pleaded. "I came all the way down from Buffalo on the train last night just hoping to get acquainted with Mr. McLendon. That's all." After looking at me for a moment, she said, "I'll see what I can do," and disappeared into the newsroom. When she returned she said, "Come along, he'll see you for a minute." This was my first inkling of politeness at the *Herald Tribune*.

McLendon, a dark-eyed, heavyset man, was friendly, but reserved. He wasn't terribly interested in what I had to say. It was a hard time, he told me, for reporters to find jobs. When isn't it? On the other hand, he didn't talk about job applications stretching to the George Washington Bridge. I deliberately kept the meeting brief and left feeling I was not chasing a lost cause.

I may have seen him once again in 1935, and a couple of times in 1936. At least he didn't find me a pest. I had no trouble getting in. I suspected that I aroused curiosity at the *Herald Tribune*, simply because I came from Buffalo. I was getting better assignments at the *Courier-Express*, and I anxiously put some of my clippings before McLendon, on which he cast a quick glance out of the corner of his eye. The next time I saw him was Thanksgiving week 1937. I have never been able to understand what came over him. He brightened up when I approached his desk. "Let's go over to the Greek's and have a beer," he said. The Greek's was an ordinary bar and grill across West Fortieth Street from Bleecks, a saloon that was celebrated as the after-hours club of the *Herald Tribune* staff. Over beer, McClendon told me he thought he had a place for me. I scarcely had time for elation when he inquired, "Where did you go to college?" I felt like the guy on the slab in the morgue. Of course, the *Tribune* would insist on a college degree. I explained to McLendon why college had been out of the question for me. Again, he astonished me. My answer delighted him. He beamed. This was the warmest our relationship had been. Finish the beer, he told me. We were going back to the office so he could introduce me to the managing editor, Grafton Wilcox.

Maybe the story of the Yale boys was true after all. Maybe McLendon was sick of Yale boys. Maybe I got my job at the *Herald Tribune* because I never went to Yale.

More surprises awaited me in New York. Although I saw McLendon once or twice again in the office, I never had another conversation with him. For reasons unbeknownst to me, he was fired. As grateful as I was to him for hiring me, I was at least as grateful to his successor, L. L. Engelking, another Texan, for making me understand what was expected of me on the *Herald Tribune*, and compelling me to achieve it. Engel, as we all called him, has been dead for a number of years now, yet I hardly ever turn on the typewriter without a sense of him looking over my shoulder, as stern about the last sentence of an article as about the first. Errors scalded him. For the pages of the daily paper he coveted the accuracy and sophistication of the *New Yorker*, a weekly magazine. One morning, I heard a genuine howl at the city desk as he was scanning the day's paper. When I glanced over, I saw him beating one of his assistants about the head and shoulders with an unlighted cigar. On the obituary page he had found a story datelined "Hoboken, N.Y." I never understood New Yorkers' contempt for Hoboken, but at least they were willing to let New Jersey keep it.

In 1982, I heard that the *Buffalo Courier-Express* went out of business. When I left there, I sensed that the city of Buffalo lacked a tradition of journalistic excellence. At times it also lacked a sense of civic taste. In the Depression years of the early 1930s a shelter for homeless men, which had been built near the old Erie Railroad Depot, came to be called the Hotel de Gink. A more contemptuous disregard for the cruelties of the Depression could hardly be imagined.

2

My Friend Fiorello

From a distance, it had long seemed to me that any New York reporter assigned to cover Mayor Fiorello H. La Guardia had two on the aisle every day. From one hour to the next in the thirties and forties, no one knew what the pudgy man in the wide-brimmed black fedora might do or say. This was the case not only in New York but also earlier in Washington, where he was a member of the House of Representatives from upper Manhattan.

In the House in the 1920s, La Guardia was the rascally leader of the "Wets," the faction fighting for repeal of Prohibition. He once took his bar utensils out on the front steps of the House side of the Capitol and defied the law by making and drinking home brew. His recipe was a mixture of malt tonic and near beer, which the dictionary defines as one of several malt beverages that are similar to beer, but have an alcoholic content of less than one-half percent.

The Anti-Saloon League demanded La Guardia's arrest. But in New York on July 17, 1926, with advance public announcement, he walked into a drugstore at 95 Lenox Avenue, near 115th Street, and purchased a bottle of malt extract, 3.5 percent alcohol, and a bottle of near beer. When a policeman walked past, La Guardia challenged him to arrest him, but the officer moved on.

Rapid fire characterized La Guardia's style as mayor. A visitor recalled watching him respond to a batch of letters by tossing them one after another to a secretary, barking, "Say yes," "Say no," "Throw it away," "Tell him to go to hell."

A city councilman from Brooklyn worked himself into a state of high indignation one day over the absence from the grounds of a Brooklyn public school of an American flag to inspire patriotism. He let it be known that at the next meeting of the city council he would introduce a resolution condemning Mayor La Guardia and calling for funds for a flagpole. When Brooklyn awoke the next morning Old Glory was waving over the school grounds. At La Guardia's orders a crew worked during the night to install a flagpole, leaving the councilman speechless.

By January 1942, the *Herald Tribune* had assigned me to cover City Hall. Late one afternoon I was still in the pressroom when the office called with a tip from our bureau in Albany, the state capital. The word was that La Guardia at that moment was meeting with the leaders of the state legislature in the Engineers Club, then on West Fortieth Street near Fifth Avenue. January was an anxious time for the mayor because it was when the legislature decided how much money the city of New York and each of the other cities in the state would receive as their shares under the new state budget.

Walking from the subway to the Engineers Club, I was stunned by the cold and hoped I could stand in the vestibule until the meeting ended. At the sight of a doorman in a monkey hat, I knew my chances were slight. A reporter inside the club to interview someone? Out!

I had barely survived an hour in the cold when, from inside, two men approached while a black fedora moved between them at shoulder level. La Guardia was only five feet and two inches tall. Once during a group picture a photographer asked him to stand up. "I *am* standing up, goddammit," he retorted.

On spotting me outside the Engineers Club, he scowled and maneuvered to avoid me. His tactic in such a situation was not to walk straight to the car, but first to slant one way and then, when I managed to get in front of him, to slant in the opposite direction. If, at some point, I did get in his way, he lowered his head so I would have to duck under the wide brim of his hat to look him in the face. In any event, we zigzagged to the car—an ordinary, two-door police squad car. It was wartime, and he often used this instead of the mayor's four-door limousine, as an example to all drivers on saving gasoline in wartime. On reaching the car, he plowed through me into the front seat and told his driver, "Let's go." After my painful wait, this was too much. I set my left foot on the running board and was in the process of leaning inside when, as the car rolled forward, La Guardia slammed the door, driving the point of it just below my right cheekbone and ripping a gash in my cheek. As the car pulled away, the mayor glanced out the window and saw blood flowing between the fingers of my glove as I tried to stanch the wound. The pain was like a stab. Even in that agonizing moment I thought, "This guy is afraid that I will sue him for a million dollars."

He rolled down his window and in a tone he might have used in addressing a hurt three year old at a birthday party asked me, "Did I hurt you? Did I hurt you?"

To my own amazement I replied, "You almost killed me, you son of a bitch."

"I didn't mean to," he protested.

"Since when can't a reporter question the mayor of New York?" I asked.

"But there's nothing I can say about this meeting," he replied. "Nothing has been settled yet." Then he brightened up and asked, "Would you like a good story?"

"What the hell do you think I've been standing out here freezing for?" I replied.

"Do you know what I am going to do tomorrow?" he inquired, eager to buy me off.

"What?"

"I'm going to announce that we will tear down the Tombs Prison."

The Tombs, a way point for many of the worst criminals of the age, was an ugly, high-rise jail facing Foley Square in downtown Manhattan. Its demolition had long been sought.

"And you know what I am going to do with the bars on the windows?" La Guardia persisted.

"What?"

With a note of pride: "I'm going to give them to the war effort."

When I entered the newsroom at the paper, smeared with blood, almost everyone jumped up. A first-aid kit was brought to me as I related what happened. From the files came a photo of the towering Tombs Prison to accompany my story in the Late City Edition. The next day, I received a ten-dollar bonus, a token of newspapering in the 1940s. There was no inclination in the city room for a story on my injury. I didn't want one. The mayor had apologized. If we reported the incident, other papers would follow suit. I am sure the mayor was pleased not to see reports to the effect that he had "attacked" a reporter. At some point later, one of his assistants approached me at City Hall and inquired if I would like to have the job of secretary to the Fire Department. *Me*? Not only was the idea unbearable, but I knew La Guardia would fire me within weeks. Such dismissals were not a rarity.

The mayor fired so many people—time and again in the case of the demanding but powerful parks commissioner, Robert Moses—that dismissals often failed to make news. One that fascinated City Hall was that of a man I'll call Jones, a member of the mayor's staff. One day the mayor summoned him. No one knew why, but Jones was fired. There were two ways out of the mayor's office: the conventional palm room through which visitors came and departed, and a long, narrow room that housed not only the telephone switchboard for City Hall but also switchboards that communicated with the entire municipal government. Five or six women operated the boards from high chairs.

Suddenly out of a job, Jones, a handsome, well-mannered, quiet man, left through the switchboard room. With his right arm arched over their heads, he walked slowly behind the women, disconnecting every single call then in progress throughout the municipal government of New York. Soon afterward he was commissioned an officer in the navy. Anyone who could respond to Fiorello La Guardia as coolly as that would be a good man to have aboard.

After Germany's entry into the war a serious problem for the Allies was posed by enemy submarines lurking in Atlantic waters beyond New York's harbor. At night the submarines could see outbound vessels silhouetted against the glow of the city and attack them. At one point, the Germans were sinking American shipping in the Atlantic at a rate faster than the vessels could be replaced. The situation urgently required a blackout of New York.*

The system had to be prepared section by section—first the Bronx, say, then part of Queens, and so on. La Guardia, of course, made himself a big part of it all. When a section of the Bronx was to be blacked out, he sent me a message asking me to accompany him on the nighttime inspection tour. I met him inside the bare entrance to his apartment house on upper Fifth Avenue, and we headed for the Bronx in the mayor's limousine. The mayor and I sat in the back seat. He didn't say anything, and neither did I. It was interesting, of course, driving along and watching the lights go out, as mile after mile of streets darkened. Finally, we returned to his apartment house. I thanked him and said good night as he disappeared silently into the building. Our next venture into darkened streets would be very different.

The blackout drills made war seem closer to New Yorkers. During the blitz we had read about the blackout of London. Now it was our turn, but without a blitz. Citizens' interest mounted as the continuing local tests approached one that would require an instant blackout of the entire city. When the time arrived there was a good deal of excitement. This night the mayor himself would choose the moment to darken all New York, and he would do it from his car. Again he invited me to join him, but this time he was on edge. He was in command. He was thrilled. As we set out, again toward the neighborhood of Yankee Stadium, he told me he would order darkness at 9:15. He and I occupied the rear seat. To the right of the driver in the front sat the mayor's police aide, Captain Hartman, who lived in constant terror of his boss. All was silence as we awaited La Guardia's order. Promptly at 9:15 he commanded the

---

* New York did not adopt a permanent, complete blackout, which would have caused serious disruption and doubtless more crime. Authorities settled on a "dimout," in which only the bottom halves of outdoor electric lightbulbs were blackened. This kept the city running fairly normally at night while reducing the glow feared by the navy. The dimout, however, was invariably referred to on all sides as a blackout.

captain to call a special number at Civil Defense, which La Guardia had given him the day before, and declare that the mayor ordered the entire city of New York blacked out. Instead of instant response there was a pause. Right away I suspected trouble. "Goddammit, make the call!" La Guardia shouted. In what must have been a state of near paralysis, Hartman was fumbling in his pockets. The mayor yelled something like, "Hartman, obey my orders!" Without looking back the police captain said he had left the number at home. To get it he would have to call information at Civil Defense. The scene in the limousine was equivalent to a blitz, American style. With New Yorkers in all burroughs waiting tensely for the lights to go out, the mayor was roaring, the driver was uncertain exactly where to go, and dead silence enwrapped hapless Hartman. I was seated so close to La Guardia I feared that if he should explode, my draft board, then on my heels, would have to look for somebody else. Quite expeditiously, Civil Defense information gave Hartman the right number, and out went the lights of New York.

I never found myself alone with Mayor La Guardia again. Before I left for basic training at Camp Croft, South Carolina, I had wanted to drop by City Hall and say good-bye. But my time was consumed with getting my wife and our six-week-old daughter settled. I did receive a letter from him in Germany later, but in such circumstances as I could not have imagined. I only had time to read the first line or two, but, as will be seen, that said it all. After the war ended and I had returned to the *Herald Tribune* in early 1946, he was in a hospital near death.

3

HOW A REPLACEMENT GOT INTO COMBAT

With thousands of other infantry replacements, I crossed the English Channel in mid-August 1944 on an aging British troop ship bound for Normandy—specifically, Omaha Beach. Mercifully, we would not have to land in the face of the enemy fire that had bled Allied forces two months earlier on D day. Yet, the moment I set foot on the vessel in Portsmouth, in the south of England, I was sure I was on a course that would lead to foxholes, as befit my Military Occupation Specialty of rifleman and my rank, at the age of thirty-two, of private, first class.

Portsmouth's harbor was alive with activity. Barrage balloons swayed on high above ships' masts. I was eager to take it all in, but abruptly we were herded below to enclosed decks with only bare floors to lie on and little illumination from a few electric lightbulbs strung about. To no effect, an irate GI yelled up a stairway, "Turn the lights on, you Limey bastards." By coincidence, I found myself next to an ill-tempered Texan whom I had also stood beside several weeks earlier on the trans-Atlantic British troop ship *Queen Elizabeth*. We were then at a railing one evening, gazing at a magnificent imitation mountain range of pink-streaked white clouds rising from the horizon. I asked him if he had ever seen a more glorious sight. "Very perty," he replied, "but I wouldn't give ya a nickel fer it."

As we eased out of Portsmouth Harbor, the hick launched an unimaginably scatological attack on Eleanor Roosevelt. Why? Because, preposterous as it may seem, she was responsible for his being shipped to the battlefields against his wishes. Periodically, he would interrupt his harangue to recite a sarcastic couplet often heard among GIs in Europe at that time, scorning Franklin Roosevelt for American involvement in the war. The Texan relished mimicking the president's tone and delivery in the lines,

I hate war.
El-ea-nor hates war.

(The statement "I hate war" had been in the speech Roosevelt delivered at Chautauqua, New York, in August 1936.)

Early the next morning, we were free to leave our dungeon. I scrambled up to the top deck to watch the low-lying Normandy coast glide by on our starboard side. Before long, we approached the man-made harbor built to facilitate the D-day landing. When our ship dropped anchor we were ordered to scramble down ropes into an already partially filled landing craft. Once aboard it, I was astonished to encounter my best friend from Camp Croft days, Sam Rappaport, a Cleveland businessman. Sam was a pure delight. He hated the army, but with reason. His legs were inadequate to his frame. Basic training was often a torment to him. He was very patriotic, however. I doubt he ever brought up the question of a discharge. As we headed into Omaha Beach I was awed at the sight of it. As long as the United States exists, this expanse of sand will be sacred. I felt it. The moment seemed to call for, "Once more unto the breach, dear friends, once more," or "I shall return," or "Give me liberty or give me death." Sam splashed ahead onto the beach, where a noncommissioned officer was directing traffic. "Sergeant," Sam asked, "where is sick call?"

In the movement of replacements Sam and I were routed to different outfits. Later, I heard that he saw some very hot action but endured it well. After the war, when I lived in Washington and he in Cleveland, we renewed our friendship. When he heard in 1978 that I had been invited by the Israeli government to speak at the dedication of the Harry Truman Library at the Hebrew University in Jerusalem, he came to Washington to give me a yarmulke—a white one. I wore it. I was saddened to hear a few years later that Sam had died.

When we replacements landed on Omaha in mid-August the fighting had moved far inland because of German retreats. On the heights above the beach and the large enclosed enemy gun emplacements that American bombers had failed to destroy, I was called to a desk, checked in, and handed the Indian-head arm patch of the Second Infantry Division, a highly regarded regular army unit. The insignia was welcome after the months of anonymity in training camps in the United States and England. With the Indian head on your arm you were somebody in the army; the Indian-head patch was a source of pride. The division would play a crucial role in Europe. General Dwight D. Eisenhower, the Supreme Allied Commander, would record that in the forthcoming Battle of the Bulge (now known in history as the Battle of the Ardennes), the Second Division met "the issue with great skill and determination and during the ensuing three days fought one of the brilliant divisional actions of the war in Europe." If brilliant, it would also be very rough.

Once those of us who were joining the division had finished the required paperwork, we were hurried into a waiting army truck and given the wildest ride of our lives—of mine anyhow. In every village, we raced through crowds that cheered us on. It was as if the fate of France depended on our getting to the front on time. Even without our knowing where we were going, the adventure was unusual and exhilarating. We were thundering along a Red Ball Highway, something I had never heard of before. Three years earlier at the landmark army maneuvers in Louisiana, it was discovered how efficiently trucks ceaselessly on the roll could deliver supplies and reinforcements to troops that were also on the move. After the Normandy invasion, the Red Ball system was imposed on main roads in France, with trucks kept moving twenty hours a day, usually in one-way traffic. That afternoon, I and the other Second Division reinforcements were whirled from Omaha Beach into a beautiful field outside the city of Rennes. Food was ready for us. Tents dotted the landscape. I yearned to settle down for a vacation. But not for long. Word got about that we would board a train that night, but we wouldn't be heading westward, where the bulk of the Allied forces were racing to capture Paris and break through the German line along the Seine. Rather, the Second Division was attached to the VII Corps for a sweep eastward across the Brittany Peninsula to capture various ports, particularly Brest on the Atlantic. The slow train was made up of old coaches with no lights. Apprehension and uncomfortable seats made sleep difficult. It was still dark when the train ended its run near the town of Landerneau, a few miles from Brest. For the first time, I heard the booming of artillery in the distance. As we trooped along, machine-gun fire rattled in a nearby woods. At what appeared to be a headquarters, we just sat down and waited for much of the day.

Early in the afternoon, a jeep was driven into the field where I sat and parked in a corner. A uniformed man got out, spread a white sheet on the hood, then produced candles and candle holders, along with religious objects and certain vestments. He was a Catholic chaplain preparing to say mass and offer holy communion. Perhaps fifteen or twenty men who were about to brave the battlefield and who could find solace in prayer and sacraments assembled around the jeep for the service.

Next, we replacements were again gathered in front of the headquarters, where a weather-beaten sergeant major welcomed us in a speech that was juvenile. The colonel in command, we were told, was a great figure. With "all that steel flying around out there," some of us were bound to be hurt, but on hand were the finest medics to treat us, and so on. I thought it would have been better if he had just spoken a couple of sentences, such as:

"The reason you men are here is that the national security of the United States would suffer gravely if Hitler overran all of Europe, which he is trying to do. Let's get going!"

Obviously, whatever reorganization was required by the arrival of replacements would not occur until the next day. But, having been greeted by the sergeant major, were we now in combat? I wondered.

From where we were standing, only a single-lane dirt road ran through in the direction of Brest. I gravitated along it a short way to the entrance to a field that was obviously a company headquarters. Dusk had fallen. The place was illuminated slightly with lanterns placed on the ground. A jeep was backed up in the entrance while the driver gathered pots and pans that had been brought in for evening chow. As I slid around it into the headquarters, I heard a captain calling to the driver. "Corporal," he asked, "have you got room for a body?" I was in combat. Truthfully, I could not believe it.

In the days after the Normandy invasion, much was made, rightly, of the hedgerows that impeded attacking Allied ground forces. But Brittany was filled with hedgerows, too. The dirt mounds themselves were five or six feet high, and on top of each of them grew a row of sturdy bushes perhaps another five feet in height. The result was a mosaic of walled fields that opened into one another or into a road. One of these fields connected with the one that held the company headquarters. A friendly sergeant, spotting me as a replacement waiting around with no place to sleep, told me to make myself comfortable in that adjoining empty field. So there it was, my own domain. In the gathering darkness, I walked about it before pausing to examine the hedgerow at the end of the field, facing enemy territory. There were some small gaps in the elevated bushes, and dug into the bottom of the dirt mound was the first foxhole I had ever seen. It appeared to be about six feet long and three feet deep. When, nearly exhausted, I settled into it, I found that the previous user had shoved in nearly enough hay to make a mattress. I fell asleep quickly and woke up in terror. Two enemy shells came screaming into the field. Two deafening explosions painted my whole world scarlet. If I had still been ambling about, I would have been cut to pieces. When all was quiet again, I dozed off, but a noise of some sort awakened me. I looked up. Standing on the hedgerow above me was a German soldier. Before leaving England we had been familiarized with the enemy's uniforms, and I had no doubt that he was indeed German. I was such a novice, however, that it never occurred to me to grab my rifle and shoot him before he shot me. He had already begun making his way down into my field, but now with his hands raised over his head. Immediately following him over the hedgerow were two GIs, one of them with a gun pointed at the German's back. Whether he was captured or voluntarily surrendered I never knew, but that trio marching off my field was the sweetest sight I have ever seen in my life.

The next morning, with little discussion, the reinforcements were formed into two platoons. Not knowing what to expect, we were marched along that same single-lane dirt road. Our rifles were now loaded. We could hear firing up ahead. I had no idea what we were going to do. As we rounded a curve in the road, a German machine gun in a ditch was pointed straight at us with a gunner in a camouflage uniform bent over the sights. Motionless. He was dead. He was a young man with blond hair and tanned cheeks. We paused. As I looked at him, it occurred to me that his parents did not know he had been killed. But now it was daylight, and every hour would bring the news closer to them. They would hate us. Would it ever occur to them, I wondered, that no armed Americans would have been moving along toward their son's post that day if Hitler had not, preposterously, declared war on the United States?

In the aftermath of the Japanese attack on Pearl Harbor on December 7, 1941, I had stood by the wire service printers in the *Herald Tribune*, reading in astonishment about Hitler's declaration. Did he understand what he was doing? Such was the lingering isolationism in America that President Franklin D. Roosevelt could not have committed U.S. troops to Europe without a deadly challenge. As it was, his request to Congress to accept a state of war with Germany was approved without delay.

The histories I read after the war explained Hitler's miscalculation. For one thing, he was ignorant of the power of American industry rapidly to produce the planes, tanks, trucks, weapons, ships, and guns needed for a successful invasion of Europe. With sheer misjudgment, he concluded that the Japanese attack would absorb the United States in a war in the Pacific, giving Germany adequate time to achieve its aims in Europe. Instead, Roosevelt decided to make the war in the Pacific a secondary effort until the Western allies and the Soviet Union had defeated Germany.

The second day of our attack on Brest revealed the spectacular side of modern warfare. Around noon our headquarters—and all others in the field, no doubt—received orders from a higher command to pull our lines back fifteen hundred yards for safety. In midafternoon seven hundred American planes would stage a bombing raid on the city. We were only a few miles from the target, so the raid would be theater for us.

The first intimation of attack was a throbbing in the air to the north of us. Then the hum of motors. Then multiplying specks in the sky. Soon the sky seemed full of bombers and fighters. In front of the planes the sky began to fill with polka dots, explosions of shells from German anti-aircraft guns. As the bombers drew closer, it appeared that curtains of soot were sifting down from them. What looked like soot from afar was in fact bombs. Small clouds of smoke were rising from the city. We could hear blasts. The anti-aircraft fire was furious. Although the planes were flying through a polka-dot sky, all of them kept coming. The big bombers were shepherded by fighters—Lightnings. The Lightnings were diving with guns ablaze to silence the anti-aircraft batteries. Directly in front of us a Lightning took a fast dive. The pilot obviously miscalculated the distance between himself and a four-engine bomber flying ahead of him at a lower level. The Lightning sheared the tail assembly off the bomber and then, trailing black smoke, went twisting and turning and tumbling into the distance exactly as depicted in every war movie I had seen since *Wings*. I could not tell exactly where the fighter struck the ground. Worse still, I could not see a parachute. The bomber seemed to stand still in the air for a moment, then went into a huge cartwheel tumbling toward the ground. I frantically looked for parachutes. None appeared. The ground I stood on shook when the bomber crashed, immersed in a tremendous ball of flame and black smoke.

The German position in Brittany was hopeless. Brest fell on September 19. In the next day or so, I was able to walk through its streets, aghast at the seas of rubble and the missing roofs and facades. Down by the piers I noticed Germans doing carpentry work and strolled closer to see what it was. They were making coffins.

Units of the Second Division were pulled out of Brittany and again taken to a railhead, this time to board a freight train to Germany. The accommodations were not those of the Simplon-Orient-Express—the floors of the boxcars had only wisps of straw left on them. Still, the freight train provided a good opportunity for seeing the European landscape. It was slow and made many stops, and we often could get out and walk around. Things that were worth looking at did not rush by. Passing at low speed near Verdun, for example, we could make out an overgrown outline of the trenches of the First World War, a more horrible one for the infantry than the war we were in. I recall a boxcar discussion about how long Europe could endure the massive destruction and bloodshed of terrible wars. After three or four days, the train let us off at what seemed to be a staging area near a city, probably Malmédy.

The next day, the Second Division moved up to occupy German soil in a wide front along the Siegfried line, a zone of enemy defensive fortifications. With alternating woods and rolling fields, the scenery of our new position was beautiful, the sunshine illuminating the autumn foliage. No farmhouses were in sight, and any civilians who had lived in nearby villages had left. Day after day our sector was quiet except for occasional firefights, touched off by patrols. At least we could tell where the German front line was by watching our artillery spotter plane, which constantly flew back and forth above it.

At the time I did some wandering myself, the very thought of which was to haunt me for years. When we arrived in Germany, I encountered another friend from Camp Croft, Joe Cobb of Baltimore. He was now a machine gunner and with two or three comrades was stationed well forward toward the German front. They had dug a pit just where the woods touched an open field, giving them both invisibility and a line of fire against any invaders. Their situation was always tense.

Joe was a smoker. In the circumstances, he smoked heavily. The carton of cigarettes the army gave each of us every Monday was gone for Joe by the middle of the week. Since I did not smoke, once every week I made my way up to his position and gave him my carton. Accordingly, one afternoon I walked along the fringe of the woods to the pit in which he used to sit behind his gun and close to his buddies. This day the pit was deserted. The long interval without any fighting had lulled me. With utter mindlessness, I stood and looked at the pit. Where was Joe? Since I had not seen anything else like the pit on the way up, I guessed it had been decided to move the machine guns forward, still closer to the German lines. I started forward again until, thirty feet or so later, the truth staggered me. The machine gun post had been abandoned, and every step I took brought me closer to German gunners. If they wanted a prisoner instead of a corpse, they almost had one. I scrambled into the woods and made my way in fright along the fringe to safety.

I never was able to give that carton of cigarettes to Joe. After he had been brought back to his base, a mortar shell struck close by, and a fragment severed his right leg at the knee. After the war, Joe came to see me in Washington. He said that when he was hit he flung both arms in the air and spun around and fell, almost exactly the way the movies portrayed collapses of the wounded in no-man's-land in the First World War.

Our battalion headquarters was in the farming village of Schlausenbach, at least half a mile back from the front lines. In the heart of the village stood what I took to be a genuinely medieval Catholic chapel of gray stone with a few front steps and a formidable wooden door. In the lock was a large wrought-iron key. Holding it would be a fistful. The moment I saw it I longed to have it. Movies of the 1920s especially were filled with scenes of castles, which had keys just like the one in Schlausenbach. I had looked with disgust on the impulse of some GIs for wartime souvenirs, most of which were junk. In my frame of mind those days, I never wanted anything in my house that would remind me of Germany. The key, however, was not junk. It would have been a precious paperweight on my desk. The more I saw it the more I wanted it, so finally I took it before the next soldier could get his hands on it. I knew that in the years ahead I would cherish it. Into my duffel bag it went.

Three days later, I saw a gathering of GIs in the heart of the village and joined them to learn what was going on. A Catholic chaplain had come down from regimental headquarters to say mass, but he couldn't get into the chapel. What I had to do was obvious. There was no decent evasion. I got the key out of my duffel bag and gave it to the grateful chaplain. After all, I could get it out of the lock some other time. But I never saw it again. In our apartment in Washington stands a decorative round table. I hardly ever pass it without thinking how splendid the Schlausenbach key would have looked on it.

We remained in the quiet sector until winter set in. In mid-December 1944, the Second Division swung north to attack the dams on the Ruhr River in Germany. The reason was that any Allied forces moving through the Ruhr River valley could have been isolated if the Germans opened the sluices. The Ruhr River dams I never saw, however. A far greater crisis arose. We were not the only troops on the move. After his terrible losses in the east to the Russians and in the west to the Allies in France after the Normandy landing, Hitler was in desperate straits. In launching the ground war in 1940, he had surprised the British and the French by driving unexpectedly through the hills, forests, and streams of the Ardennes, an area of France bordering on Belgium. Caught by surprise, the British were temporarily forced from the Continent at Dunkirk, and the French surrendered.

Now in a crazy gamble to save his regime, the Führer, with intense secrecy, moved his best remaining troops up to the fortified German West Wall in the region of the 1940 German route through the Ardennes. This was, incidentally, about the same point that units of the Second Division, including mine, had reached on their advance. Hitler was confident (and Eisenhower was concerned) that if the Germans could break through our lines in the Ardennes, they could cross the Meuse River, then turn north in Belgium to seize the inland port of Antwerp, which was vitally necessary for Allied supplies. In his memoir *Crusade in Europe*, Eisenhower stresses the importance of the Ardennes.

On December 9, I wrote to my sister, Katherine, in New York:

> It is very wintry here again with snow covering the ground and the pines. The war is in a very rough, grim stage. What a Christmas this is going to be! At this point I almost feel that I can read the hearts of all of the soldiers who have fought in all the wars of the last 1,000 years. As I just asked Marth [my wife] in a letter, how *did* the world ever come to such a pass as this? The tension, as we reach the climax of this incredible struggle, has a tight grip on us all. I wonder when it will end?

Late on December 15, the group I was with camped for the night under fir trees in a sparse woods surrounding a road junction in the Ardennes. Clumps of snow accumulated on branches. If you brushed against shrubbery, you would find your uniform wet. By nightfall, it would be frozen. Evening chow was early. By five o'clock darkness had set in. Unless you were on special duty, there was nothing to do but crawl into your cold foxhole for a long, bleak night knowing nothing of what was happening only miles away by the German West Wall. By that time, the German force ready to spring at us was equivalent to twenty-four divisions. Commanding the attack would be the famous field marshal Gerd von Rundstedt. At some point, perhaps early on December 16, when I was in my foxhole, unaware, the poised German troops were read a call to arms from von Rundstedt:

> Soldiers of the West Front! Your great hour has arrived. Large attacking armies have started against the Anglo-Americans. . . . You carry with you the holy obligation to give everything to achieve things beyond human possibility for our Fatherland and our Führer.

At 5:30 on the morning of the sixteenth, I was awakened in near shock by an enemy artillery barrage unlike anything I had ever experienced. The ground on which I lay trembled. It was the start of the Battle of the Ardennes.

Eventually there came a pause in the bombardment. In the lull, a morning chow line was formed. When I got there, I found that mail had arrived also. I grabbed a letter and breakfast and hastened back to the edge of my foxhole. To my surprise, the letter was from Fiorello La Guardia. "Dear Donovan," he wrote, "I am still fighting the punks and the tinhorns." I was sure he would rather be fighting the Germans, with the rank, say, of brigadier general. His letter was long, but I never had time to read more than a few lines. Another terrible barrage erupted. This time orders were being shouted to us to get out. The German ground attack was threatening. I dropped the letter in the snow. To our great disadvantage, the weather was gray and foggy, eliminating what otherwise would have been a priceless opportunity to turn the air force against the enemy on the ground. I was no warrior, but I felt that, having come this far, we ought now to stand and crush the Germans who were charging through the woods to smash us. Of course, I did not know that up and down the West Wall they had marshaled the equivalent of twenty-four divisions. Everyone in the midst of the Battle of the Ardennes was caught up in the frenzy. All I knew was what I saw.

The first thing of note to me was that at the nearby crossroads the commander of the Second Infantry Division, General Walter M. Robertson, whom I had never seen before, was personally directing traffic and vigorously waving us toward a road out of the forest. This was surely a sign of great urgency. In places, the snow was hip deep. Plodding through it in a winter uniform with a rifle and a heavy backpack was an ordeal. The field in which we eventually emerged was wide and reached as far ahead as one could see in the fog. An unusual phenomenon was that, in contrast to the whiteness of the area we were leaving, this untraveled snow-covered field was charcoal gray, evidently the result of the explosions of countless German shells. In this connection, I was to observe in the continuing battle that, vast and frightening as the German shelling was, it did not seem to hit the mark, to destroy our vehicles or guns or kill individual soldiers. I was nearly an exception to the last, however.

After trudging through the field for thirty minutes in a spread formation, we paused for a rest. Most of the others sat down in the snow. However, I happened to be standing next to a medium-sized haystack. With all my gear, I spread my arms out and flopped back into the straw. I could not have been more luxuriously comfortable in a Paris hotel. Suddenly a terrific explosion went off behind me. It must have been a German shell. What else could it have been? The haystack reacted by heaving me and my

How a Replacement Got into Combat

equipment, face forward but uninjured, into the snow. In any case, it was a reminder that the Germans were after us.

As we moved on, the field brought us to twin farm villages, Krinkelt and Rocherath, where our troops occupied the empty houses. In the one into which I ducked for shelter, officers and men of all ranks from private to major were thrown together. Our situation seemed so grave that only an imbecile could have imagined a sudden outbreak of cheers, laughter, and backslapping, yet it happened. In the downstairs room was a stairway to the attic. For whatever reason, a soldier, Jack Holmes from St. Louis, climbed it. As he reached the top, a shell hit the roof. A piece of plaster nearly two feet across dropped on him, yet he was unharmed, except for a bleeding cut in his left wrist. The reaction in the room was immediate.

"Look," someone yelled, "Holmes gets a Purple Heart."

He did indeed receive the decoration awarded to military personnel wounded in action.

I cannot remember the sequence of events for the rest of that day or for the next day. I do have vivid recollections of alarming moments.

While I and the others were still in the same farmhouse, a German tank rolled into position at the upper end of the village, commanding a view of the dirt road that ran between the two rows of farmhouses. Gunfire could be heard everywhere. Needless to say, not all of the Second Division was in that village. Most units were deployed in the surrounding landscape to contain the German advance. After the Holmes celebration, the major I had noticed in the house earlier summoned me to find his jeep driver and bring the driver back to the house. It was an order I had to obey, but it was outrageous and a risk of my life. In such chaotic circumstances, why had the driver not been ordered to stand by? I didn't even know what he looked like, let alone where he might be in that bedlam.

When I slipped out the front door, trying to evade any armed foe, the view was appalling. A farmhouse across the road was burning. Sparks were flying about in the darkness. The enemy tank down the road was firing rockets through the village. Some of them got into the ruts in the dirt road and streaked along like fiery snakes. For the major to try to get away from there in a jeep, if such was his intention, would have been suicidal. Seeing no one in the road, I crept around to the rear of the house. The area looked deserted. Evidently, the driver had found shelter. Lest the major think I had not searched far enough (wherever that might have been), I got out of harm's way for a while, huddled in a cowshed—the sole occupant. In due time I managed to get back into the house alive. "I cannot find your driver anywhere, sir," I reported to the major. "It's very rough out there." He was angry, but dropped the matter.

"I am mighty lucky to have come through that German offensive unharmed," I wrote my sister several days later. "We were bombed and strafed. The Germans hurled rockets at us, shelled us heavily, yet here we are."

Of course, we did not know it, but General Eisenhower had made a decision that would affect our lives. Instead of viewing the enemy attack in the Ardennes as a disaster, he saw it as a great strategic opportunity. Rather than standing and engaging in one massive battle, the Allies made a grudging, fighting retreat, inflicting casualties and destroying enemy tanks, trucks, and supplies while slowly giving ground. Meanwhile, Eisenhower summoned available Allied units from the north and from the south to form lines to hold the German attack in a fairly narrow corridor. Eventually, Hitler's forces could advance no farther under such bombardment. In the end, they retreated, and the Allies, in stages, followed them straight back into the heart of Europe.

In retrospect, we in the Second Division, and others as well, stood in those bitter December days and nights at a climax of the war in Europe. In compliance with the Eisenhower strategy, General Leonard T. Gerow, then commanding the V Corps, called General Robertson and ordered him to disengage from the battle around the twin villages—a treacherous maneuver—and move the Second Division several miles north to occupy a section of the Elsenborn Ridge. This ridge stood on the critical northern flank of the battle area, and its unforested slope would make it perilous for the enemy to attack us, once we got there. If the Germans could break through, no Allied reenforcement was positioned to keep them from seizing Antwerp, Hitler's main objective at that point. The Germans did not break through our lines.

Getting away from Krinkelt-Rocherath on the night of the seventeenth had its own drama. For the move to Elsenborn, a long line of trucks and jeeps was formed on a road leading north. I was in one of the forward trucks. We were in range of the German artillery; the sooner we could move the better. As the delay continued, emotions soared along the side of the road where the snow was deep. Powered by rage, Colonel Chester Hirschfelder, commander of the division's Ninth Infantry Regiment, came running and stumbling and yelling to the forefront to find out what was causing the stall. A lieutenant told him that a jeep, the leading vehicle, would not start. "The jeep won't start?" the colonel yelled. "Get me ten men." That was easy. The jeep was lifted and heaved over an embankment. Then we set off without interference to the Elsenborn Ridge.

The place was a different world—no incoming shells; no casualties; no prisoners. Nearby stood large unoccupied barracks that the division could use for its own purposes, including communications. Chow was at regular times, not just on the run. We were able to clean up and rest and even to take walks along the roads. Above all, the weather was clearing. The picture had begun to change on December 23, when some American planes joined the battle. Christmas morning was exhilarating. With a steady roar, hundreds of American bombers paraded across a clear blue sky toward Germany to isolate Hitler's forces in the Ardennes by bombing roads, bridges, and supply depots.

Standing in a field alone for nearly an hour watching our bombers passing overhead reassured me that Hitler, whose armies in the east were suffering terrible losses at the hands of the Russians, was finished. Compared with the harsh road from Normandy to Elsenborn, the road ahead from Elsenborn to Czechoslovakia would offer us a chance to feel like tourists. This was especially true after the Ninth Armored Division on March 7, 1945, seized intact the Ludendorff Bridge across the Rhine at Remagen. Such was the sweep of the German collapse that as we moved through eastern Germany into Czechoslovakia we spoke not of taking towns or facilities but of liberating them. Rolling into the Czech city of Pilsen, I was riding on a half-track, a vehicle larger than a jeep with wheels in the front and, in the rear, tracks such as a tank runs on. Appearing on our left was a tidy structure with tall wrought-iron and gold-filigree gates. It was the Pilsen Brewery. "Turn in, turn in," I shouted to the driver. "Beer!" He did. We pushed open the gates and proceeded cautiously lest some armed enemy fugitives were hiding in the place. None appeared. On a dock stood two barrels of beer. As we loaded them on the half-track and took off, I made it plain to the others that this was my great moment of the Second World War. I was the liberator of the Pilsen Brewery. The acclaim prevailed, even though the contents of the barrels was undrinkable. The stuff was like stale water.

On the morning of May 8, for whatever reason, I was riding on a truck along a country road east of Pilsen. If my mood was typical of the time, I was thinking about getting home to my family and back to work on the *Herald Tribune*, dwelling particularly on the promise of the managing editor that I could fill the first opening in the Washington bureau. I wanted very much to work in the capital. All of a sudden the radio in our truck came on. The essence of what we heard was this: Attention all commands. By order of the Supreme Allied Commander: CEASE FIRE. The truck stopped.

We had expected some such message soon, but the impact was unimaginable: Joy. A new world. A new life. Death no longer lurking. I was so excited, I jumped off the truck and landed in a ditch. The ditch was full of wildflowers.

My bouquet was, at my request, a transfer to *Stars and Stripes*, the army newspaper in Paris. Not having enough points to go home before Thanksgiving, this gave me six months of rehearsing for a return to the newspaper business. It also enabled me to work at night rewriting for the *Paris Herald Tribune*, for which a much-needed $700 check would await me in New York.

Leaving my friends of many months, who I probably never would see again, I was reminded of some of the experiences we had shared. I recalled the late April afternoon when our advance brought us to an overnight stop at a town in eastern Germany, the name of which I can't remember. When we came to a halt in the dirt road that ran through the town, I jumped off the half-track on which I was riding and carried my gear into what appeared to be a public building in which we would spend the night. Just before entering, I heard an explosion and saw what I thought was a chunk of the eaves falling from the front of the building next door. I was startled by the thought that from somewhere nearby German artillery was firing at us. What I in fact had seen was an American soldier in his death throes from a land mine. He had been riding in the half-track or a jeep behind the vehicle I was on when the mine blew him into the air. Riding ahead in approximately the same dirt lane as he, we couldn't have avoided the mechanism that triggered the mine by more than a few inches. Why was he killed while I was not? There is no answer to such a question.

The fact that I had avoided the explosion filled me with a strong sense of irony whenever I recalled the fate of a friend from the *Buffalo Courier-Express* days, whose name was Paul W. Dearing. A fellow reporter then, he got a job in New York after I did. While I was with the *Herald Tribune*, Paul was hired to do publicity for the War Relief Services of the National Catholic Welfare Conference. A pleasant, mild-mannered man, he became visibly upset when I told him I was about to be drafted. He visited our apartment one Saturday morning and pleaded with me to appeal to my draft board for an exemption because of my wife and our baby daughter, Patricia. He talked almost passionately about the dangers of war. He told me I could be killed. I let him talk on, but there was no way I could, or should, have escaped the draft. My draft board had already given me a two-week extension to resettle my wife and daughter. Finally, there was nothing else to say, and Paul left the apartment in apparently genuine concern that I might be killed.

After the German surrender, when I was working as a reporter at *Stars and Stripes*, I was walking along the Champs-Elysées on the way to the office one day, never feeling better. I had come through the war without a scratch. My eye was suddenly attracted to a newsstand, where a shocking headline reported that an army plane had crashed into the Empire State Building in New York. Barely able to visualize such a scene, I burst into the office and grabbed the wire copy.

The story was this:

At 9:45 A.M. on Saturday, July 28, 1945, an army B-25 bomber, bound from Bedford, Massachusetts, to Newark, New Jersey, and flying too low in fog, crashed into the seventy-ninth floor of the Empire State Building. The floor was occupied by the offices of the National Catholic Welfare Conference. The body of Paul Dearing, who probably had thought he was in the safest place in the world, surely in contrast with the army, was found on a ledge twenty or so floors below. Whether the impact of the bomber had blown him through a window or whether a fire that had been ignited forced him to jump was uncertain.

The end of the war offered a wonderful time to absorb the grandeur of Paris. A deep sense of relief permeated the city. With gasoline not yet available for civilian use, one could safely walk up the middle of the Champs-Elysées or any other thoroughfare without encountering traffic. In the mornings, I used to swim in pools along the Seine, beyond which I could see the ornate bridges over the river and towering behind them the gothic mass of Notre Dame Cathedral.

I had arrived in time to attend Paris's formal welcome to General Eisenhower, the triumphant Supreme Allied Commander. It was the first time I had seen him, although as a GI I had admired him from afar. That summer the *New York Post* published an English-language daily in Paris. The headline on the morning when Eisenhower and General Charles de Gaulle rode in an open car from the Arc de Triomphe down the Champs-Elysées read "PARIS WELCOMES IKE." Looking over my shoulder at the curb was a handsomely dressed, attractive middle-aged woman. "Pardon," she said, "is it 'Ick' or 'Ike'?"

Seven years later at the Republican National Convention of 1952 in Chicago, where Eisenhower and Senator Robert A. Taft of Ohio were contending for the nomination, I remembered the day in Paris and wondered if the American people were ready for a President Ick. For President Ike, they were ready indeed.

One experience I had in Paris left me with the enduring realization that all future peoples would confront a world that would not be the same after the lovely summer of 1945. Nearly every day I took a walk in the Bois de Boulogne, a beautiful park in Paris. As I was leaving one August afternoon, I passed a newsstand. One paper had a large headline: "LE BOMB ATOMIQUE SUR LE JAPAN."

4

Getting to Know Washington and Franklin D. Roosevelt's Proper Choice

The jarring news of President Franklin Roosevelt's death from a cerebral hemorrhage in Warm Springs, Georgia, on April 12, 1945, had reached the army in Europe the next morning. I was shaken and saddened but not surprised, because photographs in *Stars and Stripes* had showed the president gaunt and weary after the Big Three (United States, Great Britain, and the Soviet Union) conference at Yalta in the Crimea. A telltale sign was visible on March 2 when, in reporting to Congress on the conference, he spoke while seated at a table rather than standing at the rostrum.

In the group I was with, a GI, reacting to Roosevelt's death, suddenly called out, "Hey, Wallace is president now." Everyone around seemed to nod. They were wrong.

"No," I said, "Wallace isn't president. Senator Truman is."

I was greeted with a certain scorn. What the other soldiers remembered, obviously, was that Henry A. Wallace, an Iowa liberal, especially strong in the farm states, had been vice president beginning in 1941. Preoccupied with military training and the war, the GIs forgot that Roosevelt chose Truman as his running mate in 1944, despite the Missouri senator's reluctance.

What a sequence of exceptional presidents! Franklin D. Roosevelt and Harry S. Truman.

Since I did not become a Washington correspondent for the *Herald Tribune* until 1947, after the war, I knew Roosevelt only through newspaper and magazine stories and his own words on the radio, including his famous "Fireside Chats." Strange as it may seem in the age of television, the older means of communication could be very intimate. In 1933 I went to a friend's house to hear the broadcast of Roosevelt's first inaugural address. We need not "shrink from honestly facing conditions in our country today," I listened to him say. "This great nation will endure as it has endured, will revive and will prosper.... The only thing we have to fear is fear itself—nameless, unreasoning, unjustified terror which paralyzes needed efforts to convert retreat into advance." Coming from a home in gloom, I found those words decidedly encouraging. As the days went on, I viewed Roosevelt as a great president who raised our hopes and spirit. Roosevelt did not end the Depression. The war and the tidal wave of wartime construction and mobilization would do that. However, a word we had not heard in a long time—*prosperity*—began to trickle back into conversations, though not my father's.

Still broke in the prewar years, my family was headed toward the dreadful prospect of being put out on the sidewalk for not paying off the mortgage. As Roosevelt had helped farmers, laborers, and veterans of the First World War, he also saved us middle-class, nonunion city people from ejection through the enactment of the Home Owners Loan Act, authorizing the refinancing of mortgages at lower cost. It enabled us to hold on.

One day, when I was still working for the *Buffalo Courier-Express*, the managing editor stopped me in a hall and, with obvious disgust, said: "I've got to give you Saturdays off, too." A five-day week! And with no cut in pay? I was amazed, not to say elated. The new government policy on weekly working hours, which changed American commerce and society down to the present day, grew out of Roosevelt's recovery programs. In a time of enormous unemployment, the aim of the five-day week was to entice employers to hire more people to do the work of those who now had an extra day off.

It is hardly surprising that in November 1944 I voted for an unprecedented fourth term for Roosevelt. My vote was cast in the aforementioned village of Schlausenbach in the depth of war and only half a mile from the German lines. All American servicemen and women, on land and on sea, were given absentee ballots. The official tally of the election was 432 electoral votes for Roosevelt and 99 for Thomas E. Dewey.

During the remainder of the war in Europe, few of us had any concept of President Truman. Even after the war, when I returned to the city staff of the *New York Herald Tribune*, I heard different views. My own opinion began to form after my transfer to the paper's Washington bureau. Although I was assigned to cover the Senate, I went to the White House for all of Truman's press conferences.

It was the custom then for a bureau chief to introduce a new member of his staff to President Truman after a White House press conference, and that is how I came to know him. He was friendly and unassuming. In appearance, he did not match my naive concept of a statesman but rather seemed an ordinary, successful, neat, well-established, sixty-two-year-old American. In the left lapel of his gray double-breasted suit was a First

World War army discharge button (he had been a captain in the artillery), and on his left hand he wore a gold Masonic ring. His mention of the *Herald Tribune* when we met had a caustic note, but it was inoffensive because I felt he was referring to the editorial page's orthodox Republicanism on domestic issues. What struck me most about him was the power of his handshake. It took me a while to recall that he had spent years behind the plow as a dirt farmer.

As the 1948 presidential election campaign approached, millions of dirt farmers in the Midwest would hear from that fellow from Missouri. Their response would astound the world.

In the meantime, I had been introduced to the hazards of dining out in Washington. Like many a new Washington correspondent, I was shown the press table in the Senate Dining Room, an inviting scene. The chandelier in the center of the room, conforming with the simple Colonial Revival style of the place, was installed between 1910 and 1915. Most of us would have been more interested in knowing when Theodore Roosevelt King had been installed as the waiter for the press table. King, a former dining-car waiter, was a slight, nimble African American, surely the best waiter in the Western Hemisphere, the most polite man anywhere, and one whose solicitude for his patrons exceeded that shown on the Senate floor. King's profuse bowing would better be described as bobbing and was perfectly synchronized with his rubbing of his hands together in eagerness to serve. If he did not know your name, he addressed you as "Mr. Bzzzzzz."

I dropped by the table soon again, even though I had not yet met the reporters who were on hand. King was waiting on a man across from me who I was told was Tris Coffin, a columnist on the old *Washington Times-Herald*. By the time King returned with his order, a woman had slipped into the empty chair on Coffin's right. After serving him, King took the woman's order, which, fittingly enough, included the renowned Senate bean soup. I had never seen her before, nor have I seen her since.

When King brought her lunch and returned again to the kitchen, she rose from the table, unobtrusively, picked up the bowl of thick, piping-hot soup, and poured it over Coffin's head. For those of us on the opposite side of the table, the spectacle was paralyzing. Coffin, dressed in a dark suit with a shirt and tie, sat motionless as the bean soup trickled from his hair, ears, and nose and drained off under his collar. King, reentering the dining room, froze in his tracks at the sight—but only for a moment. His head bobbing up and down and his hands twisting around each other, he darted to the victim, asking, "Is there something wrong with the bean soup, Mr. Coffin?"

Word went around that the woman, a freelance photographer at the Capitol, felt insulted at a reference to her in one of Coffin's columns. After the bean soup drama, there were reports that her credentials to the House and Senate press galleries were lifted.

The Senate Dining Room was not the only venue for hazardous dining in Washington. On an Indian summer day in the mid-1950s, I had a luncheon date with Thomas E. Stephens, one of President Eisenhower's principal political advisers. When I picked him up at the White House, I inquired, as usual, "Is this a brown suit day?" "Blue," he replied, "but it's bad enough anyway."

A native of County Dublin, Ireland, jaunty, keen, trim, and good-looking, Stephens had faith in his powers of perception and applied them to the president's moods. In due time, he concluded that Eisenhower's temper was worst when he wore a brown suit. Every morning Stephens would watch out the window to observe the president walking from the White House proper to the Oval Office in the West Wing. When he wore a brown suit, Stephens would spread through the White House the warning, "Brown suit day!" Eventually, while talking to the president on a blue-suit day, Stephens confided his theory. It was his impression that thereafter Eisenhower wore brown less often.

In the beautiful weather, I told Stephens that I wanted to take him to lunch at a new garden restaurant on Seventeenth Street, barely a five-minute walk from the White House.

"No," he replied. "I hear the food there is terrible."

"Not so, Tom," I said. "I've been there. The food is okay."

Stephens, a victim of ulcers, demurred. I had no trouble arguing with him since we were old friends, dating to City Hall days in New York when he was a political adviser to the Republican president of the city council, Newbold Morris. On a day like the present, I felt it would be good for Tom to sit out among the shrubs and flowers for a change. The restaurant was set off from the sidewalk by a wrought-iron picket fence and gate. We were within several feet of the place, our argument ended, I thought, when the gate suddenly slammed open and a man burst out and threw up on the sidewalk.

We lunched at the Hay-Adams.

Perilous dining in Washington is not necessarily confined to restaurants. Banquets, even as high up on the scale as the annual spring dinner of the renowned Gridiron Club, have their misfortunes. The club's spring dinner is strictly white tie. For elegance, I cannot forget the one worn at dinner some years ago by John Hay ("Jock") Whitney, variously multimillionaire, sportsman, socialite, publisher of the *New York Herald Tribune*, and President Eisenhower's ambassador to the Court of St. James's. Whitney was the guest of Roscoe Drummond, a *Herald Tribune* columnist. As a former president of the club, Drummond sat at the head of a long table, with Whitney on his right. During the evening, of course, he talked with the guest on his left also. Drummond was a bubbling, gesticulating conversationalist, and in one of these discussions he drove home a point with a sweep of his right arm, only to knock a glass of red wine down the front of Whitney's stiff white shirt. It looked as though the ambassador had been hit by a bazooka shell.

The management of the Statler Hilton, where the dinner was being held, was summoned to action. Whitney was accompanied from the room while the manager found a key to a men's shop on the ground floor. He returned with the best dress shirt he could find, which could not be compared with the one now soaked in wine. Whitney put it on without the least show of distress and returned to the dinner to enjoy the skits. After the dinner, he joined many of the other guests and members in a reception given upstairs by Cowles Publications in Suite 1240.

The rooms were almost crowded when he arrived, but he and a friend found space on a couch. Behind it at shoulder height was a table with some highballs on it. At that moment, Geoffrey Drummond, Roscoe's son, forcing his way through the crowd, bumped into the table and knocked a highball down the back of Whitney's neck. Stunned again, he turned around. When he saw Geoffrey standing there, he declared to his friend, "I'm never coming to a Gridiron dinner with the Drummonds again."

The political campaigning style of Harry Truman was new to me. At the outset, the term *whistle-stop* was new to everyone on board the president's train. It had been introduced in so many words by Senator Robert A. Taft, the son of the late president and subsequently chief justice of the United States, William Howard Taft. Addressing the Union League Club in Philadelphia, Senator Taft accused Truman of "blackguarding Congress at every whistle station in the West." Reaching for political gain from Taft's remarks, the Democratic National Committee telegraphed officials of thirty-five cities and towns on Truman's itinerary to ask how they liked being called "whistle-stops." The tactic was provocative because the term was railroad parlance for communities classified as too insignificant to enjoy regularly scheduled train service. The term quickly took hold as the enduring description of Truman's style of campaigning.

Truman confided to Henry J. Nicholson, the Secret Service man who was close to him, that he would rather run against Governor Thomas E. Dewey of New York, the leading Republican contender, than against Taft. A scrapper, Taft was Truman's keenest critic. The senator's wife, Martha, was believed to have coined the gibe "To err is Truman." Other quips from that direction were "Harry Truman for Governor" and "Two families in every garage." Notwithstanding, Truman would carry Taft's home state of Ohio in the election.

In the campaign Americans by the millions, including reporters, editors, and publishers, believed the public opinion polls when they said that Dewey had a commanding lead. The respected Roper poll ceased operations in mid-September on the grounds that Dewey was a sure winner. A former district attorney of New York, Dewey was a hard-boiled prosecutor of indicted criminals. As a campaigner, he was more subdued, more formal, and, of course, more guided by the polls than was Truman. Harry Truman was an acknowledged admirer of "Mad Anthony" Wayne, an impetuous, hotheaded general on George Washington's staff in the American Revolution. At the start of the 1948 campaign Truman was ready to lay into Dewey and the Republicans, especially the Republican-controlled Eightieth Congress. The campaign train proved an ideal vehicle for carrying his fight into the crucial states.

In those days, campaigns did not begin a full year ahead of time, but a forerunner of Truman's 1948 fall campaign already had provided sparkling copy in mid-June when he was invited to deliver the commencement address and receive an honorary degree at the University of California at Berkeley. He made the "nonpolitical" round trip in a special presidential train. When I arrived for departure at Union Station at 9 P.M., my first view of the train was comforting. Tables in two brightly lighted dining cars were covered with crisp white linen. A bouquet of fresh flowers graced each table. The railroads on the route had sent their best conductors, best waiters, best porters, and best chefs to service the presidential train. There was a club car and bar, of course, for the press. Each reporter had his own stateroom. There were two work cars for reporters. Each of those cars had planks at windowsill level, running nearly the full length of the car on both sides. Each reporter had plenty of room on the planks for his typewriter and papers. In effect, each had his own window. At each end of the cars was space for mimeograph machines to produce texts of the president's speeches. There was also a space for Western Union, which transmitted the reporters' copy to their respective papers.

The last car on the train was the Ferdinand Magellan, reserved for the president and his family and guests. It was just a few steps from the chairs to the rear platform from which the president spoke to the people who came to see him at each stop.

By the time he reached the West Coast, President Truman had called the *Chicago Tribune* the worst newspaper in the country; the *Tribune* retorted, calling him a nincompoop. He called the Republican Eightieth Congress the worst Congress since the days of Thaddeus Stevens, a leader of the radical Republicans during Reconstruction. Representative Cliff Clevenger in Washington called the president a "Missouri jackass." Senator Taft went on the radio and proposed that Congress adjourn until a new president was elected. From the balcony of the Elks Club in Bremerton, Washington, Truman said, "You know, this Congress is interested in the welfare of the better classes. They are not interested in the welfare of the common man, the everyday man."

"Pour it on, Harry!" someone shouted.

"I'm going to. I'm going to," he replied.

Then it was time for him to return to his train and head for Berkeley for his commencement speech. His last appearance of the day would be at the railroad station in Eugene, Oregon. No text had been prepared. His talk would be impromptu. The train would not be in Eugene long enough for anyone to file a story there. And from then on until the next morning in California there would be no stops other than a service stop for the railroad people to check things. We could have a long evening in the bar car, or so it seemed. When the train arrived in Eugene we all filed out at the station to listen to the impromptu remarks. They astonished us.

Whatever caused the president—in a remote corner of Oregon—to allude to the postwar conference in Potsdam in Germany the previous July was puzzling. The principals at the conference besides Truman were Winston Churchill and Joseph Stalin.

"I got very well acquainted with Joe Stalin, and I like old Joe," Truman told the people of Eugene. "He is a decent fellow. But Joe is a prisoner of the Politburo. He can't do what he wants to. He makes agreements and, if he could, he would keep them. But the people who run the government are very specific in saying that he can't keep them."

What was this all about? What a story! "Old Joe" Stalin was one of the most terrible men in human history. A prisoner of the Politburo? He was a slaughterer of men around him.

The press car was in an uproar, with reporters demanding that Western Union move their stories. But how? As soon as the speech was over the train pulled out of Eugene. Slightly less than an hour ahead was the service stop. Carroll Linkins ("Linc"), the faithful Western Union representative who traveled with us wherever we went, pleaded that he had only a single telegrapher at the service stop. The man would have been overwhelmed trying to move forty or so stories. Watching Linc's expressions convinced me that all of this was futile.

I went to my typewriter. I wrote a story about two and a half pages long on the inane "old Joe" speech and the day's other political events. Then I clipped to it a page of instructions, which read about like this:

> Please telephone, collect, the *New York Herald Tribune*. The number is Pennsylvania 6-4000. Tell the operator you are calling on behalf of Bob Donovan, who is traveling with the president on the West Coast. Ask for the national desk. When an editor answers, tell him who you are. Tell him that I had no way to move my copy by wire. Tell him that I want you to read my story to our telephone recording room. When your call has been switched, follow their instructions and carefully read this story aloud at your regular pace. When you are finished, ask telephone recording to give the story to the national desk.

Along with the story and my instructions, I clipped a twenty-dollar bill. And then I waited. The service stop was to be in a small town, the name of which I never learned. The train was to stop there for five minutes at most. I could only hope that some townspeople would be at the station seeking a glimpse of the president. My mind was made up that I would give the story to a woman. When the train stopped, the conductor let us out. There the woman stood. She was attractive, dark-haired, in her late thirties, I judged. She was nicely dressed in a green sweater and plaid skirt. When I stepped off the train, I did not look anywhere else. I approached her a little too suddenly, and she appeared startled. But, having only a couple of minutes, I introduced myself and explained my plight. I told her that I would be grateful for her help and handed her the story and instructions.

"What's this twenty dollars for?" she asked.

"I want you to have it," I said.

"I don't want it," she replied.

"I've got to jump on the train right now, or I'll be stranded," I called to her, as I raced for my car without ever learning her name.

Inside was a din of bellyaching over communications. I didn't have a doubt. When we arrived in San Francisco the next day, I called New York to inquire. The story had made our front page in every edition.

Meanwhile, certain high officials of the State Department had telephoned Clark M. Clifford, one of the president's speechwriters on the train, and pleaded with him to try to keep Truman from saying anything else nice about Stalin, which was completely at odds with the foreign policy of the United States. In any case, the president dropped the subject.

Long afterward, I heard two of Truman's highest advisers in the White House, George M. Elsey and Clifford, discuss how the Old Joe speech may have come about. Both had heard American diplomats who were at Potsdam say that Stalin was capable of being polite and friendly and was at one time and another rather gracious to Truman at the latter's first international conference. Elsey and Clifford also said that the term "prisoner of the Politburo" sometimes turned up in other contexts at White House foreign policy discussions and was familiar to Truman. The president appeared on a minor occasion at Eugene without so much as a paragraph of prepared text or notes. It was a pleasant time, the president was in a pleasant mood, so he regaled the small crowd with a brief, pleasant, but very newsworthy speech.

5

A Phenomenon

President Truman's reelection campaign in 1948 was launched in Union Station in Washington in mid-September. His running mate, Senator Alben W. Barkley of Kentucky, was on hand to cheer him and charm the ladies. When the train was about to depart, Barkley called to Truman, who was waving from the rear platform, "Go out there and mow 'em down!"

"I'll mow 'em down, Alben," Truman replied, "I'll give 'em hell."

From then on, if the president so much as went to church, he would risk hearing shouts of "Give 'em hell, Harry!" from the congregation.

Except that they took me away from my family periodically, I relished those Truman campaign trips, largely because I loved trains. Presidential trains were a treat. During the 1948 campaign, we visited Grand Coulee Dam, spent a night at Sun Valley, skirted the Cascade Mountain range, rolled through the Royal Gorge of the Colorado River, visited the shores of Puget Sound, toured California valleys, crossed the Great Salt Lake on a railroad trestle, and were immersed in the autumn foliage in Wisconsin and other midwestern states.

Although debates between presidential candidates were not yet in style, President Truman and Governor Dewey were speakers on a program to dedicate Idlewild (later John F. Kennedy) International Airport in New York. Almost no one heard him say it, but Truman whispered to Dewey, "Tom, when you get to the White House, for God's sake do something about the plumbing."

In covering Truman in 1948, I witnessed the end to an American political institution. Beginning with the Eisenhower–Adlai Stevenson campaign of 1952, with a couple of minor exceptions, candidates have campaigned by air. Using aircraft, they can travel quickly between widely separated cities and towns, and followers can rally at airports instead of at railroad stations.

Yet there was a lore about the railroad press cars that was lost in the exchange. Eddie Folliard, a delightful political reporter for the *Washington Post*, told me of a discussion he once heard in a stateroom during one of Franklin Roosevelt's campaigns. Two prominent humorists of the time were riding the train for a couple of days. Eddie was listening to them and heard them agree that the essence of American humor is nonsense. They further agreed that the funniest remark ever made by an American was by Mark Twain when he said, "I'd rather sleep with Lillian Russell with no clothes on at all than with General Grant in full dress uniform."

The train was important to Truman's campaign because the support of the unions was crucial. The number of laborers in the railroad yards across the country was far greater than that at the airports. Tom Dewey, incidentally, provided an example of how Truman could exploit this situation. As the Republican nominee began to speak from the rear of his train in Beaucoup, Illinois, one day in October, the train suddenly lurched backward a few feet toward the crowd. If the movement had continued, a serious accident might have occurred. Fortunately, it did not. But, unsettled, Dewey exclaimed into the microphone, "That's the first lunatic I have had for an engineer. He probably ought to be shot at sunrise, but I guess we can let him off because no one was hurt." The Democrats were quick to charge that Dewey had disclosed his true feelings about the workingman. A day or so later, Truman's train rolled into the yards at Logansport, Indiana, a railroad center. To the large number of trainmen on the scene, the president related what a grand trip he had been enjoying. "We have had," he said, "wonderful train crews all around the country, and they've been just as kind to us as they could possibly be." That was what the audience wanted to hear.

While crisscrossing America on the train with Truman in 1948, I recognized what was clearly a phenomenon in the land, yet I never thought to mention it in my stories. After all, my assignment was to write about Truman's campaign. Furthermore, I didn't know at that time that the phenomenon would have a name. Certainly it never dawned on me that the phenomenon was more important to the history of the country than the outcome of the Truman-Dewey campaign of 1948. The phenomenal scene was a profusion of babies. Babies were everywhere, especially in the arms of young mothers who had come to a railroad station to hear Mr. Truman speak.

In some cities and towns, the president would leave the train to address gatherings elsewhere. In particular, I remember a drive up Michigan Boulevard in Chicago, where large crowds—babies included, of course—watched him pass. In small towns, as we passed through residential neighborhoods, we saw them close by in baby carriages, on porches, and on lawns.

When they became known as "baby boomers" I do not recall. In 1948 alone, according to the Census Bureau, the population of the country grew by 3,637,000. With the ending of the wars with Germany and Japan in mid-

1945, millions of American servicemen began returning home. I should have known. Two of my own three children are baby boomers. The historic growth of the country's population was swelled also by the expansion of life spans through the advancement of medical science and improvements in living conditions.

A growing population may produce problems of one sort or another for a president. President Truman was barely affected, if at all. But even as he campaigned in 1948, a particular two-year-old baby boomer in Hope, Arkansas, named Bill Clinton, was toddling along the road to the White House where a myriad of problems springing out of population growth would await him.

The last of the whistle-stops before the November 1948 election was Mattoon, Illinois, after which Truman would wind up in St. Louis for his final speech on Saturday night. On this short run, White House Press Secretary Charlie Ross took me aside in the club car to say that President Truman wanted me to know he thought the *Herald Tribune* coverage of his campaign had been fair. When we reached St. Louis. I received a telegram from the New York office directing me to return to cover what was overwhelmingly expected to be the Dewey victory celebration, planned for election night in the Roosevelt Hotel, and then go on to Albany to be with the president-elect until he moved into the White House after his inauguration.

The doors to the Dewey victory celebration in the ballroom of the Roosevelt were to open at 7:30 in the evening. Shortly before that, the news tickers carried some early returns from Connecticut, showing Truman leading Dewey in the popular vote. I had to go down to the main lobby for some reason, and straight off I ran into the growing line of Republican fat cats, sumptuously dressed and impatient to get to the ballroom. A stout man in a tuxedo in front of the line with his wife noticed my reporter's badge and called, "Hey, press, what's this about Truman being ahead?"

"Where did you put my mink coat?" his wife interrupted to ask him.

"If Truman wins, you won't have a mink coat," he fretted.

6

WAKE ISLAND—AND BEYOND

At dawn on October 15, 1950, the press plane descended on Wake Island, which from the air looked like a small circle of sand and palm trees in the vast Pacific Ocean. We were arriving from Washington to cover an extraordinary meeting between the president and General Douglas A. MacArthur, the renowned commander of the United Nations forces in the war raging with Communist North Korea.

The war had erupted the previous June 24 when, without warning, North Korea invaded South Korea and soon came dangerously close to driving UN forces into the sea. That danger was averted when a UN armada, commanded by MacArthur, assaulted the port of Inchon and trapped the invading North Korean forces. This enabled the United Nations to advance across the thirty-eighth parallel, the dividing line between the two Koreas, in a great effort to defeat the North Koreans in their own territory. In this strategy lurked a dangerous possibility, and it was a factor in Truman's decision to confer with MacArthur. The danger was that a UN victory might spur adjacent Communist China to pour large forces across the border and, inflicting heavy casualties, sweep MacArthur's troops back over the thirty-eighth parallel, or even to defeat.

As usual, our press plane landed on Wake several minutes before the president's. All of us were eager for a glimpse of MacArthur. I know I was. I had never seen him before. As Truman's plane approached, some of us wandered about looking for the general. The resident population of Wake was so small that only about forty people were at the runway, hardly enough to conceal anyone. The president's plane landed. No MacArthur. The engines were turned off. The door of the cabin was opened. But the president did not appear. I had never seen anything like this. The curtain had risen, but the actors were not on stage.

Long afterward, when I was working on a history of the Truman presidency, Henry Nicholson, the Secret Service agent who was always at Truman's side, explained the impasse to me. I had first to recall, he said, a scene between President Roosevelt and MacArthur in Honolulu on July 26, 1944, during the Second World War. Roosevelt had arrived aboard the cruiser *Baltimore* and invited MacArthur and other high-ranking army and navy officers to a reception on the quarterdeck. Before cheering crowds on the deck, the guests arrived, all except MacArthur. After a long delay, MacArthur came roaring onto the dock in an open car escorted by motorcycles with sirens blaring. Striding up the gangplank, he paused to acknowledge an ovation from the spectators, then greeted President Roosevelt.

President Truman did not arrive at Wake Island ignorant of the scene at Honolulu.

"Have to talk to God's right-hand man," he had written to a cousin before the trip.

Once the president's plane had landed on the Wake Island runway, Truman and Nicholson went to the open cabin door. After scanning the scene, the president returned to his seat. He said MacArthur was still sitting in a jeep behind a group of people. Truman told Nicholson the general was not going to upstage him the way he had upstaged Roosevelt. The president settled down to wait. Then, without our noticing it, MacArthur slipped through the small crowd and stood in a welcoming posture at the bottom of the landing ramp.

Truman emerged and walked down the stairs.

"I've been a long time meeting you, general," the president said.

Without saluting the commander in chief, reporters noticed, MacArthur replied. "I hope it won't be so long next time, Mr. President."

Surprisingly or not, the relationship between the two men that day was friendly. First, they talked alone together. Then they joined in a combined session with the government officials who had accompanied each of them. As the morning wore on, we pressed Charlie Ross on how we could get the news out of these sessions. Could we, for instance, interview the president and the general together. "There is no plan for that," Ross said. Indeed, his replies about the availability of news were increasingly pessimistic, as if his announcements would be quasi communiqués: "President Truman and General MacArthur met today and discussed the Korean War situation." All the way to Wake Island for a communiqué!

Later in the morning, one of us happened to glance up a rise in the land where there was a small shack with a little balcony. Standing alone on the balcony was General MacArthur. Apparently, there had been a short break in the talks. Three of us scrambled to the shack. The general knew we were there, but kept gazing above us. One of us asked if he could he tell us about his talks with the president. "You'll have to ask the president's press agent," he replied. The title would not have appealed to Charlie Ross, whose official

Wake Island—and Beyond

title was press secretary to the president. Press agents work on Broadway. We persisted, however, because if we were going to get a good story, it would have to come from the general. All was futile until we heard footsteps behind us. It was a colonel coming briskly to talk to MacArthur. Although it was a Sunday on Wake Island, it was Saturday in the United States. The colonel walked up the steps to where MacArthur was standing, saluted, and leaned toward him. We pressed forward to hear him. We were especially interested in hearing anything about strategy discussed with the president.

"It's Army 7, Michigan 7 at the quarter, sir," the colonel said.

The general thanked him and returned to the meetings. In a few hours we were on the press plane bound for Washington via Honolulu. It was largely a silent journey. Our offices had sent us halfway around the world for news. There was no news. Nothing was changed. The origins of the meeting were curious. The year 1950 was a time of off-year elections. Reverses in Korea hurt the Democrats. The idea of Truman's going to the Pacific to confer with MacArthur took root in the Truman staff, with George Elsey in the vanguard. Charles S. Murphy, special counsel to the president, said the proposal carried the day because "it was good election-year stuff." Comments at Wake Island by Truman's staff, such as the one that MacArthur may have tried to upstage the president, must be read in light of Murphy's comment.

Not since the Japanese attack on Pearl Harbor in 1941 could I recall such an alarming time for the United States and the UN allies as the end of November 1950. A long-dreaded menace exploded on November 25, when three hundred thousand Chinese Communist troops attacked MacArthur's forces in the northern region of Korea and began driving them back. "We face an entirely new war," MacArthur said. He had not believed it would happen.

On the morning of the thirtieth, more than a score of reporters, including myself, were lined up in the White House waiting to be admitted to a presidential press conference. Ordinarily, when the president was ready for us he was apt to say, "Let the goons in." This day there was no fun inside or outside the door. At worst, the Communist invasion could lead to a third world war, with the Soviet Union allied with China against the Western powers.

The president opened the conference on a practical note. "The United States," he said, would "rapidly increase its military strength." His request to Congress would "include a substantial amount for the Atomic Energy Commission, in addition to large amounts for the Army, the Navy, and the Air Force." In the tenseness of the moment, the routine reference to atomic energy laid the groundwork for a confused press conference and ensuing upheaval abroad. A usually assertive president made some inept answers. Without being specific, he said, "We will take whatever steps are necessary to meet the military situation, just as we always have."

Then came a question from a young *New York Daily News* reporter: "Will that include the atomic bomb?"

I believed at the time that this was a show-off question. Truman was nowhere near a decision to drop an atomic bomb on North Korea, yet his answer was ambiguous.

"That includes every weapon we have," he said.

Certain newspapers around the world went haywire.

Il Momento, in Rome, reported that bombers were ready to take off from the United States on one hour's notice. "No! No! No!" pleaded *The Times* of India. British Prime Minister Clement R. Attlee quelled fear in Parliament by flying to the United States to discuss the question of the atomic bomb with Truman. After friendly talks, Attlee confidently returned to London.

On Saturday morning, December 2, two days after the disturbing press conference, Truman and his entourage arrived at Union Station to take his special train to Philadelphia for the Army-Navy game, a presidential tradition. Charlie Ross had confided to me the day before that, in view of the alarm over Korea, sudden cancellation of the president's trip might cause panic.

As was characteristic of presidential trains, the Pullman cars had separate accommodations for each passenger. Mine was a single compartment, not far from a stateroom at the end of the car that was soon crowded with photographers and reporters playing poker. With my door open, I loafed until we passed Baltimore. Then, I took up my typewriter and worked on the body of a story I would file from Philadelphia after the game, with a quick lead on the president's day in a time of crisis.

Since my door was open, I did not hear anyone enter. Suddenly, I sensed a presence and looked up to see President Truman standing there, watching me in amusement. I jumped up and shook his hand. As the two of us stood close together in that small place in the train, I had a new appreciation of his good looks, friendliness, and vigor. I cannot recall what we talked about, but it was not momentous. Then he said good-bye and headed for his own car. His departure at that particular moment was to lead me into an intense dispute with the White House before the day was over.

One of the nearby poker players was Robert G. Nixon, the eccentric White House correspondent of the old International News Service, a lesser rival of the Associated Press and the United Press. Nixon happened to look up from the game and espy the president leaving my compartment. He was dumbfounded that Truman was walking through the train and fearful that he had already talked with AP and UP reporters aboard. Nixon scrambled out of the stateroom and burst in on me, demanding, "What did he say? What did he say?"

I not only resented such an abrupt intrusion while I was working but also could not believe that Nixon would think that in the crisis overhanging him President Truman would make a newsworthy comment to me or to any other reporter. I was so galled by Nixon's stupidity that I replied off the top of my head that Truman said, "Take to the hills, men." My recollection is that this was a line bantered about in high school, perhaps picked up from an old Tom Mix or Hoot Gibson Western film. It is not cited in *Bartlett's Familiar Quotations*. Still worried about what the other wire services may have picked up from Truman, Nixon departed.

A loner, Nixon died some years ago. Although I used to see him around press rooms every day, I knew little about him. He was a natty dresser, attached much importance to himself, and was addicted to slot machines when any were around, as in Key West, where President Truman used to vacation. Nixon was a mite haughty to those who did not share his opinions.

One night at Key West when the president was vacationing there, authorities revealed that someone had smuggled a jackass into the navy yard where he stayed and tied the animal to the shower stall on "Truman Beach." We all let fly with this story—all but Nixon, who had had one or two too many and was asleep in a bedroom in the Bachelor Officers Quarters, site of the presidential press headquarters. Carroll Linkins responded to Nixon's absence. Linc asked a reporter for one of the news magazines to write the story for Nixon to keep him out of trouble with the home office. I cannot remember the reporter's name, but he was one of the best writers. When Linc had the copy about the jackass, he thought he had better show it to Nixon to let him know what he had done. A couple of us accompanied him and found Nixon asleep on a top bunk. Linc woke him and explained why we were there. Nixon sat up straight, stared for a time at the copy, then slowly tore the pages in half. "*This* is a *travesty* on my style," he declared, and plopped back on his pillow. Linc filed the story to INS and saved Nixon a good deal of embarrassment.

The game in Philadelphia was very exciting. Navy won. On the trip back to Washington, the importance of the Chinese crisis dimmed in the warmth and chatter of a club car. When I got home at eight o'clock, my wife told me the White House was trying to reach me and wanted me to call the press office as soon as I returned. I suspected a new development in the Korean War situation.

The last thing I could have imagined was hearing that INS had put out a bulletin, available to many radio stations, as well as certain newspapers, quoting President Truman as saying at the height of an international crisis, "Take to the hills, men!" How did I learn this? From Charlie Ross, on the telephone, in a tone so angry he could hardly speak. What this indicated to me was that the president was even angrier. Ross had called INS in New York to protest and traced the quotation to me. I was caught between outrage and a sense of total absurdity. There was too much sarcasm around press rooms in those days. Now, I was guilty for blurting out words Truman never uttered.

My most urgent problem was to get Ross, a fair man and a former journalist of distinction as Washington bureau chief of the *St. Louis Post-Dispatch*, to understand what had happened in my stateroom. I told him I was sorry—an understatement. On the other hand, I refused to accept the blame for the news bulletin. I did not file such a story to the *Herald Tribune*. I regretted what I said to Nixon, especially the thoughtless wording on such a day. But no responsible reporter would ever have filed such a statement attributed to the president without first verifying it with White House officials. What Nixon did was a deliberate piece of mischief.

"I can't be blamed, Charlie," I protested. "You know Nixon. You're steamed up now, but when this settles, you'll understand."

And so he did, especially since the bulletin did not cause panic. Ross never held a grudge against me. I have no reason to think Mr. Truman did either. What surely would have amazed him and me at the time would have been the many future years of research and the hundreds of book pages I devoted after his death to the history of his presidency.

7

Harry Truman's Hearty Departure

During the time of the postwar Potsdam conference, President Truman took a ride in Germany with two of the great generals, Dwight D. Eisenhower and Omar N. Bradley. Out of the blue Truman turned to Eisenhower and said: "General, there is nothing that you may want that I will not try to help you get. That definitely and specifically includes the presidency in 1948." "Mr. President," Eisenhower replied, "I don't know who will be your opponent for the presidency, but it will not be I."

In *Crusade in Europe*, Eisenhower also remarked about Truman: "Up to that time I had met him casually on only two or three occasions. I had breakfasted with him informally and had found him sincere, earnest and a most pleasant person with whom to deal."

By the approach of the 1952 election, the general's opinion had changed. Wrote his biographer, Stephen E. Ambrose, "By November of 1952, Eisenhower actively disliked Harry Truman. He thought the president was guilty of extreme partisanship, poor judgment, inept leadership and management, bad taste and undignified behavior. Worst of all, in Eisenhower's view Truman had diminished the prestige of the office of the President of the United States."

I had never heard such an opinion expressed before. Mr. Truman was, after all, a president with a record that included the Marshall Plan, NATO, the British loan, vital Greek-Turkish aid under the Truman Doctrine, the Berlin airlift, recognition of Israel, early reconciliation with America's enemies, Germany and Italy, and, in contrast to the League of Nations fiasco of 1920, U.S. membership in the United Nations. Furthermore, Truman's chief advisers in foreign and military policy, General George C. Marshall and Secretary of State Dean Acheson, were unexcelled.

A historic landmark in the advancement of civil rights was the report "To Secure These Rights," which Truman submitted to Congress on October 29, 1947. The recommendations, familiar reform now, were to be fought over for the next two decades.

I liked Eisenhower and admired him as a man of fine character and a good president. My early impression was that his undoubted greatness in history would spring from his role as Supreme Allied Commander in the war in western Europe against Hitler. Obviously, of course, the combination of military leader and president of the United States was potent. In 1952, Truman would have welcomed Eisenhower as a presidential candidate—on the Democratic ticket. He was rankled that Eisenhower had decided to run as a Republican. John W. Snyder, who was Truman's secretary of the treasury and also his best friend, confided to me: "At bottom the president resented Ike running as a Republican. He thought he should have run as a Democrat. Truman had offered him the nomination in 1948 at Potsdam. Truman believed more could have been done for the country as a Democrat. [The Democrats] built [Eisenhower] up." The fact, or coincidence, that it was under President Franklin D. Roosevelt that Eisenhower was lifted out of near public obscurity by appointment as Supreme Allied Commander and was insured perhaps centuries of fame over the Normandy invasion and was now with certainty headed for the presidency as a Republican soured Harry Truman. In politics, as contrasted with foreign policy or military affairs or Supreme Court decisions, Truman was welded to the Democratic Party, and the result, on occasion, put a chip on his shoulder.

I covered most of the Eisenhower campaign, the outcome of which was never in doubt. As the cool weather set in, he was a striking figure in a double-breasted camel-hair coat and brown fedora. Sometimes, during a speech, he would pull an egg from his pocket and ask the people if they knew how many different taxes were on it. The crowds did not care about egg taxes but were thrilled by a hero.

I attended the Eisenhower inauguration, although I did not cover it. There was still some lively copy in the activities of the now former President Truman. After the midday inauguration ceremonies, Truman attended a luncheon given in his honor by the retiring Dean Acheson. At one point, John Snyder noticed that Truman was standing alone looking out a window. "Come and have a drink," he urged his old boss. "Two hours ago," Truman said, "I could have said five words and been quoted in fifteen minutes in every capital of the world. Now I could talk for two hours and nobody would give a damn."

A few hours later, a good many people gave a damn. Hundreds of Democrats turned up at Union Station to see Harry and Bess Truman off to Kansas City. When the two appeared on the rear platform of the B&O's *National Limited*, the crowd sang "Auld Lang Syne" and waved placards suited for a Democratic National Convention.

"I'm just Mr. Truman, private citizen, now," he told them.

I made the trip along with about five other reporters. As the train rolled west the next morning, Truman was not quite a private citizen yet. As he

Harry Truman's Hearty Departure

walked through the cars, passengers rose and waved and cheered. Sometimes, when passing staterooms with open doors, he would glance in and set off screams of excitement. At St. Louis, he stepped off the train to buy a newspaper at an outdoor stand where the proprietor and the other customers were so taken aback that sales came to a stop except for one passenger from the *National Limited*.

I have never heard of another president getting such a hearty send-off from Washington at the end of his term. The reporters traveling with him asked Mr. Truman if he would have lunch with us the day after next at the Muehlebach Hotel in Kansas City, and he accepted. In a private dining room, the luncheon inevitably turned into an off-the-record press conference. I found it wonderfully informative until a reporter from the *Washington Evening Star* scuttled the whole affair by asking Truman about his order to drop two atomic bombs on Japan. He declined to take any more questions.

We saw him off to tackle the most exhilarating and gratifying task for all departing presidents. In his case, it was the building of the invaluable Harry S. Truman Presidential Library in Independence, Missouri.

As for me, I was about to enter upon my own extraordinary and rewarding labor.

8

Inside Story

No president could have entered the White House in 1953 and found the going easy. Nevertheless, in contrast to the calamities of the Depression in the Roosevelt administration and the turbulent conversion from a wartime to a peacetime economy under Truman, the Eisenhower period was a calmer time, particularly because he settled the Korean War. Certain other events beyond his control were bound to relieve international tensions in the long run. In only his third month in office, he was stunned by the news that Stalin, the dangerous Russian dictator, had suffered a fatal stroke.

Although the Republicans controlled Congress, the conservatives and reactionaries and the scoundrel Joe McCarthy caused Eisenhower miseries. Still, the president had a grip on government policy and was very popular. By 1955, he had quietly decided to run for a second term in 1956.

After having covered Eisenhower's successful 1952 campaign, I continued as White House correspondent for the *New York Herald Tribune*, which happened to be Eisenhower's favorite newspaper.

One afternoon in the summer of 1955, I received a telephone call from Kevin McCann, a writer of speeches and messages for the president. I was surprised when he invited me to lunch and was particularly curious when he asked me if we could go somewhere other reporters were not likely to see us together. The main dining room at the Statler Hotel was such a place. When we settled down to a table a couple of days later, he immediately brought up the subject of a book on President Eisenhower. I reminded myself that the next year, 1956, was a presidential election year, harvest time for campaign books. I guessed what might be coming next. I said I would not be interested in writing a campaign book. He replied that he was not thinking of a campaign book, but rather a portrait of President Eisenhower, "warts and all."

"Are you speaking for the president, Kevin?" I asked.

"I am speaking for Governor Adams," he replied.

In 1955, Sherman Adams, the former governor of New Hampshire, was the most powerful White House assistant since Harry Hopkins in the administration of Franklin D. Roosevelt. Adams had managed General Eisenhower's winning campaign in the New Hampshire primary in the winter of 1952. In the fall, he was largely in charge of the general's election campaign against Governor Adlai E. Stevenson of Illinois. All presidents organize the White House for their own convenience. It was no surprise, therefore, when the former general created an original staff system, with Adams as its chief. "My right-hand man," President Eisenhower called him. Outside the Oval Office, Adams ran the White House. New Hampshire is the Granite State, and Adams had plenty of it in his makeup. His reputation as something of a tyrant permeated Washington. Even some Republicans in Congress resented him as a man who blocked them from seeing the president. Many of the men and women in the White House feared him but liked him. Joseph W. Martin Jr., a Republican who was speaker of the House in the early Eisenhower years, told me that Adams "received a great deal of criticism that found its way to him only for lack of another eligible target."

I liked Adams, though he was a difficult man to grasp. A month before my lunch with McCann, I had interviewed Adams for an article *Collier's* magazine had asked me to do on him. He was helpful, but probably expected to receive some more swipes from the press. When the piece appeared, leading the magazine, some people around him told me that he was surprised and pleased. That would be helpful to me if I were to have more dealings with him. However, I turned McCann down completely. A campaign book, I told him, was not my dish.

Three weeks later, he called me again and asked me to have lunch with him again at the Statler. Of course I did, and in the same frame of mind as before. This time the picture began to change. Why, he persisted, would I want to deny the *Herald Tribune* the kind of material the White House was willing to offer? Had I considered how valuable such material could be to the *Herald Tribune* Syndicate? Indeed, I had not. He went on to say that a former college professor on the White House staff, Arthur Minnich, had, from the beginning, taken notes on meetings of the Cabinet, on staff meetings, and on meetings with the Republican congressional leaders. I would have access in full to these; I could talk to anyone in the administration I wished to; the White House would consider giving me any documents I might request. These statements would have caused any reporter to have second thoughts. I asked McCann if I could talk to Adams. The next day, I was in Adams's office. I thanked him for considering me for such an undertaking. He replied that the offer had first been made to Roscoe Drummond. Drummond explained that he could not handle his column and a book and recommended me instead. I had been in Washington for eight years. I already had a book published by Harper and Brothers in 1952, entitled *The Assassins*. Reviews were favorable, and five parts of this volume about the assassinations and attempted assassinations of American presidents had appeared in the *New Yorker*. Adams and I had worked together for the *Collier's* article. Obviously, I had qualifications he sought.

As to the proposed book, I told him that just as Drummond would have had trouble handling a column and a book, I, too, faced a practical problem. Since my beat had been the White House, I had only a reporter's general knowledge of areas such as the State Department. I did not have adequate background for diplomatic subjects that ought to be dealt with in the book in sufficient depth.

Adams's reply convinced me that I was getting into something pretty big. He would, he said, apply to the government security agencies for a highly rated Q clearance for me that would permit me to read secret and top-secret documents in a search for background. Ultimately, this arrangement did work very well. Adams stated that the project would remain in abeyance until I received the Q clearance.

I learned a deep lesson then. A Q clearance required a full field investigation by the FBI. Such an investigation gets into past episodes and places subsequently so meaningless to the subject that he or she has not thought of them in years. As time passed that summer, I began to worry. As I was soon to learn, the investigation had hit a snag. That was the McCarthy era. Suspicions came easily. I might not have been asked by the White House to explain a problem. In retrospect, I can imagine some official saying, "Let's call it off. Let's not take a chance of involving the president in this. Let's just say the president was cool to a book at this time." In such a case, I would have been deprived of an opportunity that would boost my career strikingly. Certainly, if the anti-Communist-minded, patriotic president and publisher of the *Herald Tribune*, Ogden "Brownie" Reid, were to learn that his White House correspondent had been denied a Q clearance because of certain Red connections, I might as well have gone back to Buffalo.

Fortunately, I received a call one morning to go to the White House to see a man whose name I did not learn and still do not know. Businesslike, he bade me pull up a chair to his desk, on which rested a pile of government documents. In a manner a bit stiff, he selected one and said he wanted to read it to me. In sum, it said: On April 30, 1941, Robert Donovan of New York City, registered at the President Hotel in Atlantic City. At that same time, the following Communistic organizations were holding meetings in the hotel. The list sounded like an honor roll compiled by the *Daily Worker*. Mostly, it seemed, there were left-wing labor unions, including the Transport Workers Union, headed by Mike Quill.

I listened to the man's reading in disbelief. Fourteen years before, I was in Atlantic City along with a crowd of Communists, and now a sector of the White House was tied up over it. The Transport Workers Union had threatened to strike the New York subway system. On the eve of the strike, Quill called a meeting at the President Hotel to raise a war chest. The city desk assigned me to cover it. The President was a cruddy hotel, but I stayed there, as did other reporters, to be close to the session. I supposed I would knock my White House questioner off his feet by telling him all this. Not quite. Where was my evidence? I did not get into the clear finally until the *Herald Tribune* library sent him a copy of the story I filed to the paper after Quill's meeting. I still wonder if this is the kind of trash the government stores up by the barrel with power to damage any one of us for perfectly lawful activity.

Finally purified by the FBI, I won agreement from Reid and George Cornish, the managing editor of the *Herald Tribune*, to work full time on the Eisenhower book. I had every reason to believe they were eager for me to do it. They granted me a year's leave of absence with pay and put on the Washington bureau's payroll a researcher for me, Vera R. Glaser, who was to become a highly respected Washington journalist. Then I saw Adams, and we agreed that ground rules were essential for both of us. He was firm in saying that any book page or passage based on top-secret documents must be turned over to him for a national-security review. I accepted that, although a case was to arise that would threaten to kill the book. Adams insisted that the book be published in May 1956. With my fingers crossed behind my back, so to speak, I assented, and dozens of times worked until 3 A.M. to comply. John Appleton, my editor at Harper and Brothers, the publisher, said we would discard galley proofs and go directly into pages to save time. Because of the delay over the Q clearance, however, the best we could hope for would be publication in June 1956, nine months later.

Throughout our discussion I waited, almost in anguish, for Adams to rule that the material from the White House could be read by me but not quoted. The style of the book, its readership and its impact, would depend on whether it was full of hitherto unknown but revealing quotations by the president and his advisers. Adams did not raise the point. When the book came out, the quotations did cause some shock at the White House.

Through McCann, Adams doubtless knew of my concern about campaign books, and he agreed with me that no one in the White House would see anything I wrote until the book was off the press. Somehow or other, I believe, Adams saw some pages. I resolved my own qualms on these grounds: The White House would regard this work as a campaign book. I would not. I would write it the only way I knew how, namely, as a book by an objective reporter relating events as he had been trained to see them. I would neither extol nor criticize Eisenhower.

One thing I dreaded, perhaps excessively, was that at some point Adams would arrange for me to interview the president. If that had happened, I might have felt obliged to quote in the book practically everything that he would say to me. This would have given the work the aura of a campaign book—an aura different from what I wanted. Since I had a unique mass of documents at my command, I wanted the book to be based on that kind of extraordinary evidence. Furthermore, the president was not likely to tell me much more than, in general, I knew already. I had covered his 1953 campaign, and since he had become president I had covered his every press conference and every speech. Eisenhower was very open about what he was doing and hoped to do. If it came down to a certain unclear problem, I could inquire of his staff and cabinet members. In any case, I did not talk to the president while writing the book.

9

WHO SAID JOHN FOSTER DULLES COULDN'T TELL A FIB?

Late in December, I told Adams that the top-secret documents were helping me with background in foreign policy, but I also needed a more personal touch in addressing President Eisenhower's approach. Without hesitation, Adams exerted what I considered the greatest source of his authority: "The president wants. . . ." As I sat in Adams's office, he told the operator to call Secretary of State John Foster Dulles. When the call went through, Adams said, "Foster, the president wants you to talk to Bob Donovan, who is writing a book about the administration with our assistance." Of course, I was not surprised at Dulles's reply, except that he would meet me at his home on New Year's morning. Out went any rollicking New Year's Eve celebration.

Promptly at 11 A.M. I rang the doorbell at the Dulles home, just off Embassy Row, and was greeted by a butler in a white jacket. Once inside, I heard the secretary of state's voice booming from somewhere in the distance about I. W. Harper. The butler escorted me to the large living room, at the end of which a broad staircase wound gracefully down into Dulles's study on the ground floor. "The secretary is on the telephone but will be with you shortly," the butler said, and then disappeared. No one else was in sight. Nothing about the architecture prevented sound in the office from rising to the living room.

"That I. W. Harper must come out of there," Dulles commanded. The response undoubtedly displeased the secretary, causing him to lay down a barrage of objections to I. W. Harper. As a matter of courtesy, my position was untenable. Invited to the secretary's home, I was sitting in his living room, overhearing his private telephone conversation. I tried to solve the problem by moving to the far end of the room, but there was no way of escaping his penetrating voice. Obviously, I could not wander by myself through other parts of the house. Not seeing Mrs. Dulles, I supposed she might be in a bedroom somewhere. The butler had vanished. All I could do was sit and overhear.

The situation was incredible. The soberest-looking man in the United States was hollering at someone about I. W. Harper. Why was the son of an upstate Presbyterian minister, himself a pious former official of the Federal

Council of Churches, wasting his energy on New Year's morning in a quarrel over high-priced bourbon whiskey? Was there a ruckus over a family liquor bill? Had some State Department official gone off the rails on entertainment expenses? Did it have to be settled on New Year's Day? In a flash the thought dawned on me. I. W. Harper was a code word. An international crisis was developing. Usually, nothing would have pleased me more in those days than to stumble into diplomatic intrigue. But, when Dulles discovered that I had heard a secret code word, would he cancel my appointment?

The telephone conversation finally over, the butler reappeared and said the secretary was ready to see me. I found him perfectly composed, arousing in me a sly thought that this was just the kind of pose a diplomat would strike on the verge of a momentous event. We talked for more than an hour. The interview was worthwhile. On the way home, however, my thoughts dwelt less on what he had told me than on the meaning of I. W. Harper.

A few days later, I stopped at the *Herald Tribune* bureau to pick up a book to read on the train I was about to take to New York. "If you are writing a book on Eisenhower," James E. Warner, the day desk man, said, "you'd better read this." He handed me galley proofs of an article scheduled to appear in the January 16 issue of *Life* magazine. For a variety of reasons, it was a very controversial piece written by James Shepley, the *Time-Life* bureau chief in Washington, depicting Dulles's global travels to meetings. Once in the air, returning from a grueling session, Shepley reported, the secretary could relax completely with a glass of I. W. Harper. So that was it? Dulles did not want people to know. Although I had heard him demand that I. W. Harper come out, here it was before my eyes. But only in galley proofs, of course. The magazine was due out that day. The moment I was in New York, I went to a newsstand and bought a copy. I. W. Harper did not appear in its pages. Sometime after Dulles's death, I recounted the episode to his brother, Allen W. Dulles, the amiable director of the Central Intelligence Agency. It delighted him, and he laughed as if to say, "Good old boy, Foster! That was the way to do it!"

There were other unusual experiences resulting from Adams's calls to high officials, informing them that the president "wanted" them to talk to me. None was more surprising than the case of Adams's call, at my request, to Robert Cutler, special assistant to the president for national security affairs. I thought that, under the circumstances, he might tell me something interesting. As a rule, Cutler, a Boston banker, was so adamant against giving reporters information that he regarded it as an insult if one even approached him. Adams's call transformed the man. Cutler asked that I meet him for dinner at the Harvard Club in New York. When I arrived, he had two chairs moved in front of a tall, blazing fireplace, ordered drinks, and asked how he could help me. I had some questions ready. He started talking and never stopped. He was *dying* to talk to a reporter. He began over the drinks, then continued through dinner, and finally wound up back in front of the fireplace again for a nightcap. I could not keep up with him.

At one point, he jolted me. In the midst of our talk, he expressed his own surprise at what he said was the number of people in the administration who favored preventive military action—against the Soviet Union, obviously. When I left the club finally, the thought was bouncing in my head, but I knew already I would not put this in my book. I would have to know a great deal more than could be learned before a glowing fireplace in the Harvard Club. I took Cutler at his word, but it was not enough to go on. If I had launched in a book on Eisenhower a report that preventive action against the Soviets was under broad discussion in the White House, it would certainly have been picked up by the press, perhaps causing loud reaction. Anyhow, the thought of Eisenhower's ordering preventive war against the Soviet Union, even amid the stresses of the cold war, did not ring true to me.

One disappointment of the Eisenhower files I saw was that they cast no further light on the president's feelings toward Richard Nixon. Opinions on the question differed. Nevertheless, in that summer of 1959, the country was hit by a steel strike and the president approved Vice President Nixon to represent the administration in seeking a settlement. Eisenhower's motive was probably twofold. Nixon would do a good job. If he succeeded, it would help him win the Republican presidential nomination in 1960. Nixon succeeded rather dramatically. For a considerable time, he had courted a small group of reporters he would invite to his office in a group on occasions when he wanted to talk. Because I was with the *Herald Tribune*, I was one of the members of this group. Now, he had settled the strike and wanted us to know how he did it. That was important news, no question. He said his words would be on the record and then unfolded the story. Automatically, I took it down in shorthand. Back in the office later, I called New York and suggested that we run a tight story on the Nixon disclosures, and play it on page 1 along with an exclusive full-length text of Nixon's words. Cornish agreed.

At seven o'clock the next morning, the telephone rang at home while we were all asleep. Herbert G. Klein, the vice president's press secretary, was calling. He was among the best of the people Nixon had around him. I could tell at once that Klein was embarrassed, and I remember the exchange clearly.

"The vice president," Klein said solemnly, "wants to know whether you had a microphone concealed on you yesterday."

If such a question had been asked later at the Watergate hearings, namely, whether someone taped Nixon instead of Nixon taping someone else, it would have been the laugh of the week.

"I never dreamed of using a concealed tape recorder anywhere," I told Klein.

"Then where did the text come from?" he demanded.

"The vice president's words were on the record, Herb," I reminded him.

"Yes, I know," he persisted, "but that does not answer the question of where the *Tribune*'s text came from."

"I write shorthand, Herb," I replied. He was incredulous.

Very few newspaper reporters in the United States in 1959 could write shorthand, even though portable tape recorders of any quality were years away. In 1998, I still use shorthand; it has been a godsend to me. When Mayor La Guardia once shouted that I had misquoted him, he had to shut up when I took out my shorthand notebook. As a copyboy in the early thirties, watching reporters stretching themselves into taffy trying to take down accurate notes on telephone calls, I decided there was a better way. In the mornings, therefore, I attended the two-room North Park Business School in Buffalo until I had mastered Gregg sufficiently at the hands of a good-looking, young blonde teacher.

Despite their contempt for Nixon's espousal of postwar Red-scare politics well before Joe McCarthy lighted the sky, many reporters respected the vice president for his drive and intelligence. As a rule, they did not feel as close to him as certain of them did to Kennedy or Truman or Ford or Reagan. Reporters believed that Nixon was suspicious of them, and he may well have been, if Klein's call was any indication.

Now, however, much more amazing problems were at hand for me.

10

A Newspaper Reporter Swamped in Classified Documents

For my hefty research on President Eisenhower, I was given an office on the second floor of the East Wing of the White House. It had been used by Robert Montgomery, the actor, who coached the president on the use of television, but the space was vacant at the moment. The setting, with its white walls, was very pleasant. When I arrived each morning, the White House archivists (as I supposed they were) brought me lists of materials they had in different fields. The documents I selected arrived in loaded carts. The writing of the book I did at home, on nights and weekends. So great was the volume of classified papers, I had to make up my mind early what subjects the book would address, or I would have been awash in secret and top-secret documents. Whatever I wanted, they photocopied for me.

One of the first lists, for example, consisted of documents dealing with the sale of electric generators to Great Britain. I recalled the issue but responded, "Thanks, bring up something livelier than this." I called up the Arthur Minnich notes on the Cabinet and other conferences in toto, and they proved to be the lifeblood of the book. The hours, days, and weeks alone in that office, engulfed in classified papers, were an astonishing experience for a reporter. I still wonder whether any other reporter in the history of the Republic ever found himself or herself in such a situation.

It was quite a while before I learned the most amazing part of this arrangement. According to all evidence, President Eisenhower did not know what I was doing. To be sure, his concurrent vacation in Denver had something to do with this fact. But, not until March 1956, three months before the book's publication in June 1956, did he know I was even writing it. Considering my weeks in Montgomery's office, the irony to me was that Eisenhower, when he was finally told of the project, questioned whether I had been given "exactly the same information" that would have been given to any other qualified reporter engaged in a similar task. All this is contained in a recently released secret memorandum he sent on March 12, 1956, to a friend, William E. Robinson, the business manager of the *Herald Tribune*, who certainly knew what I was doing.

"The fact is, of course," Eisenhower said, "that I do not know how the book got started and whose idea it was."

What he did not mention was that he had complained to Adams that the "story" of his administration was not getting to the people—the eternal tribulation of presidents. "When Eisenhower decided to run for a second term," Adams was to write later in his memoirs, "a few of his friends and associates suggested that I and the White House staff should cooperate with an experienced political journalist in writing a book about Eisenhower's first three years in office, something that would reveal to the public his work and the real nature of his problems as president, and display his personality and human qualities. . . . I did not consult the president about the project, and he had nothing to do with it." Adams did not explain this to me. The fact that Eisenhower did not know that I was writing a book about him with the help of classified documents would have dumbfounded me.

One day, when the end of the manuscript was in sight, I received a call at home from Adams, asking me to come to the White House immediately. When I arrived, the usher took me into Adams's office. At the table sat Adams, Dillon Anderson, the current special assistant to the president for national security affairs, and Colonel (later General) Andrew J. Goodpaster, the president's distinguished assistant on military affairs. An empty fourth chair at the table awaited me. On taking my seat, I sensed that something was amiss. It was, very much so. Anderson was aggressively trying to kill the book.

The simplified explanation was this: In his early months in office, Eisenhower adopted what was called a New Look in military policy. We reporters in the White House and the Pentagon had written about it thoroughly from a press release, but it did not make very interesting copy. Then recently, while poring through government papers, I had come upon the top-secret document promulgating the New Look. I read it. I could not see that it was different, factually, from what we had reported. It was, however, set forth in a much more interesting style than any newspaper account that I had seen, including mine. The military services are remarkably concise in promulgating orders, policies, and so forth. I based my chapter on the New Look, therefore, not on what I had written for the *Herald Tribune*, but on the document. I did not use any quotation marks, but, unwisely as it turned out, I used much of the official language. The copy was read by Anderson under my ground rule with Adams that any pages based on classified material must be submitted for clearance to the national-security agencies. The ensuing scene in Adams's office was a near crisis. Anderson was simply storming with accusations that, if published, my book, using the language of a document, would enable the Soviet Union to break the secret code of the United States. The book was a threat to national security. The book must be abandoned at once. The torrent was directed at Adams, not me. Adams shook under the barrage, but he did not yield. Suddenly, he grabbed all the papers on the desk, arose from the table, and said, "The president will have to decide this."

As he disappeared from the room, Anderson, Goodpaster, and I sat in silence. I was in panic. After all the negotiations with Adams, after all my work, day and night, after all my confidence that the book would do wonders for me, suddenly it was to be submitted for the president's judgment. How could I even guess what his decision would be? I supposed he and Adams would have a long discussion over Anderson's demand. Much sooner than I anticipated, however, Adams returned. Was it possible, I wondered, that Adams had not seen Eisenhower? But how could that be? He put the papers back on the table. "The president," he asserted, "says that the project will go on." Eisenhower, I feel certain, would have been surprised to hear it. He would have been equally surprised at how much gratitude I showered on him at that moment for what I assumed was his decision.

11

A "Most Unorthodox" Best-Seller

When published in June of 1956, *Eisenhower: The Inside Story* immediately became number one on the *New York Times* best-sellers list and remained number one for thirteen more weeks. Reportedly, fifty thousand copies were sold that summer. Newspapers were quick to pick up passages like the one noting that Eisenhower had said angrily that he would not get in the gutter with Senator Joe McCarthy. The depth of Eisenhower's exasperation with uncooperative Old Guard reactionary and isolationist Republican elements in Congress was revealed in the book in these words:

> What was the use, he demanded to know, of his trying to lead the Republican Party along a course that was progressive and forward-looking, but still clung to the middle road?
> He began asking his most intimate associates whether he did not have to start thinking about a new party.
> As he conceived it, such a party would have been essentially his party. It would have represented those doctrines, international and domestic, which he believed were best for the United States and, indeed, the world. It would have attracted those men and women of the older parties who believed as he did and who wanted to promote and preserve enlightened and progressive policies.
> The president even went so far as to think of a name for it, but never hit upon one.

Publication of my book produced headlines all over the country. Two congressional committees threatened investigations into how I could have obtained information from the White House that they could not. For several days, I appeared to be on the brink of being subpoenaed. I was mystified as to what the result of that might be. Sherman Adams had been very square with me, and I did not want him to be hurt. Did not the constitutional guarantee of freedom of the press justify a reporter's refusal to reveal the source of his information in the book? I believed it did. That was the stand I was going to take if I were summoned, which I was not.

Democrats staged their own sideshow to embarrass the White House over the book. Representative William L. Dawson, chairman of the House Government Operations Committee, wrote to Eisenhower, demanding that the committee be given the same information I was. Other letters followed.

Representative Emanuel Celler, a New York Democrat, who was chairman of the House Judiciary Committee, charged that it was "unconscionable," "irresponsible," and "shocking" for the White House to refuse information to Congress and then give "unlimited access to a friendly newspaper correspondent."

Senator John McClellan, a Democrat from Arkansas and chairman of the Senate Investigations Subcommittee, invited Maxwell Rabb, secretary of the Cabinet, to testify on the controversy. Rabb replied that "there is nothing I can add to yesterday's details" that he and his staff had given me documents for use in writing the book. That was true. McClellan then issued a statement, demanding that the White House immediately disclose "whether Congress and its committees are being discriminated against in favor of selected, preferred . . . reporters."

The book aroused all sorts of bombast. Thirty years later Richard Kluger wrote a book entitled *The Paper: The Life and Death of the New York Herald Tribune*, in which he asserted that my "vision" had been "skewed" by the paper's support of Eisenhower. Skewed is defined by *Webster's* as "to give a bias to: to distort." "The purpose of this book," Kluger continued, "was not primarily to serve posterity but to help the President get reelected and the author pay off the mortgage while pleasing his employer. None of this was an ignoble motive, but they did not add luster to [Donovan's] previously unblemished integrity."

In justice to Kluger, who was more than generous to me in most of his book, he based his case on the sound rule that a reporter should not write copy in a manner that would favor one candidate in an election. Rules have exceptions. The exception in this case was the extraordinary material that was made available to me and, therefore, to readers. This was material that years later would have been opened to scholars at the Dwight D. Eisenhower Presidential Library in Abilene, Kansas. In 1956 I was free to use this material as I pleased, subject in one rare case to alleged infringement on national security. In that instance—the Dillon Anderson protest—I won.

In the growing notoriety over the book, what did prominent critics have to say?

The June 14, 1965, issue of the *New Yorker* carried a ten-page article on the book by Richard H. Rovere, the brilliant author of "Letter from Washington." "Quite possibly," he wrote, "the most unorthodox thing the

Eisenhower administration has done to date, has been to grant a White House correspondent the privilege of examining the minutes of all its Cabinet meetings and a large number of documents involving confidential proceedings with the Executive Branch."

He continued:

> What the administration has done is more than merely to make available to a gifted and friendly journalist the materials for a report on its activities; it has given a person unconnected with the government . . . and subject to no disciplines or restraints beyond those in which any citizen is subject, the right to acquaint himself to the limits of his curiosity with transactions of a sort that have in the past been withheld, both from the courts and from Congressional committees authorized to investigate the Executive Branch and armed with the powers of subpoena. In effect, as the situation is understood here, the administration armed Mr. Donovan with his own power of subpoena and tendered a pledge to comply with his summonses, except when, in its own judgment, matters of national security were involved. And it gave him the further right to acquaint the entire American public—indeed the entire world—with the details of its affairs.

Rovere also noted that I had "not gained entrée" to White House affairs "simply in order to celebrate harmony and achievement." This meant that the book had reported exasperation, such as caused the president, briefly, to think about a new party. Rovere concluded that the book was "a unique piece of work in that it is a campaign document that provides as much ammunition for one side as for another." He characterized the book as "remarkable."

On July 1, the *New York Times Book Review* carried on its front page a review by Richard Stout of the *Christian Science Monitor* under the headline, "Day by Day Inside the White House. The President and His Administration Are Shown in Unprecedented Close-up." Stout characterized the work as offering an "extraordinarily intimate glimpse." In a passage that brought me a great sense of relief, he added: "It is hard to see how informed arguments either for or against the Eisenhower administration can be carried on hereafter without wide reference to this book." Rovere's conclusion had been essentially the same.

The early reviews of the Eisenhower book aroused debate over the propriety of the release of minutes on White House meetings. The subject was addressed in the leading editorial of the highly respected *St. Louis Post-Dispatch* on July 26. It said:

A "Most Unorthodox" Best-Seller

> The *Post-Dispatch* position on this row is that it is the Eisenhower administration's business what it does with the minutes of its Cabinet meetings. We believe that readers of the book will find the disclosures of such intense interest that they will be glad the White House opened its closed records to Mr. Donovan.
>
> [The book] is an earnest, painstaking effort to tell the American people what their government really has been like for the last three-and-a-half years. The debate over the propriety of release of official material ought not to be allowed to obscure the portrait of a president. . . . Never before has such a book come out six weeks before the nominating conventions and only four months before the next presidential election!

Eisenhower never mentioned the book to me, not even after his retirement to Gettysburg, where I used to call on him every month or so. At least I made his diary, later released with his papers. In the entry for January 18, 1954, he wrote: "In Washington today, I think certain [reporters] observe the very highest standards of fairness, accuracy and objectivity. Among them are Drummond, Krock, Arrowsmith, Clark, Lucey, Darby, and a chap named Donovan." Missing from the list were some excellent reporters.

On the whole, Eisenhower's relations with the press were very good. His prolonged climb to the top in the army had given him an intimate view of international strategic problems. He was personally acquainted with European leaders. After he resigned from the army, wealthy friends had him appointed president of Columbia University. Although he was a figurehead in that position, it made him visible as a civilian and gave him an opportunity to enlarge his grasp of domestic issues. By the time he was in the White House, he was astute in public affairs. Washington reporters respected him, especially no doubt those who, like myself, had served under him in the war. When he became president, I did witness a couple of instances in which an erstwhile general's anger was forced to the limits by reporters' questions or stories.

Before the mid-1950s, no one to my knowledge had seen helicopters on the South Lawn of the White House. Then, in keeping with Eisenhower efficiency, his staff decided it would save time if he took a helicopter instead of a limousine between the White House and Andrews Air Force Base in neighboring Prince George's County, Maryland, where *Air Force One* was regularly stationed. Coincidentally, the installation of a new system on this order came at a time of periodic squabbles over the federal budget.

During a presidential press conference on March 27, 1957, William McGaffin of the *Chicago Tribune* was recognized. McGaffin struck me as a rather easygoing man, but a bit brash at press conferences.

"Mr. President, sir," he asked, "do you feel that there are any economies that you can make in the executive branch of the government to help cut government spending? For instance, would you be willing to do without that pair of helicopters that have been proposed for getting you out to the golf course a little faster than you can make it in a car?"

I thought I could detect ice forming around Eisenhower's deep blue eyes. He did not relish questions about his golf and bridge games.

"Well," he replied, "I don't think much of the question because no helicopters have been procured for me to go to a golf course."

"Well," McGaffin began again, as if to lay out his case. He got no further.

"Thank you; that is all," President Eisenhower told him.

A couple of years earlier, Eisenhower had been infuriated over a story about himself in the *New York Times*, which was unquestionably accurate, yet not outrageous enough to shock a dozen citizens. It was, nevertheless, a good yarn that no doubt stirred vast gossip in New York the next day before being quickly forgotten. During a brief vacation in Denver in the summer of 1954, the president went trout fishing in the Rocky Mountains. As always, White House reporters followed him in case of unforeseen events. We didn't wait along the water's edge with the fishermen, but watched from a roadside higher up. To pass the time, some reporter inevitably would ask Press Secretary Jim Hagerty how many trout the president had caught. Invariably, as on that day, Hagerty's answer was, "The limit—ten." Staying within limits was in accord with Eisenhower's speeches on morality, righteousness, and obedience to law and order to keep the national fiber strong.

On the Denver trip the *New York Times* man was Joseph A. Loftus, a bright reporter who had his own techniques, one of which he applied that day, leaving the rest of us in the lurch.

When Eisenhower picked up his *Times* the next morning he was greeted with the headline: "President's Catch Exceeds Limit."

The story began:

> Denver, August 27—President Eisenhower went fishing for trout high in the Rockies today and in a few hours his catch went over the legal limit. The unofficial account on the president ran from 15 to 20—rainbows and

browns. The legal limit is ten. What other members of the party caught is unknown.

How did I know Eisenhower was furious? As with all presidential press secretaries, Jim Hagerty's words reflected the president's views. The next time we saw Hagerty after President Eisenhower's trip to the Rockies, he growled, "Do you guys know what you are going to get from now on? Shit!"

12

NO OTHER STAG DINNER LIKE IT

Invitations to President Eisenhower's periodic black-tie stag dinners were among the most coveted in Washington. To him, these dinners were of a certain value no doubt because of discussions in which he became engaged with a variety of guests, and to the guests they were elegant and unforgettable. One, to which I was invited in the fall of 1956, gave me a fresh insight into the president's thinking on certain matters that I might not have picked up elsewhere. Of course, the dinner was private, but in later days what I had learned could influence what I wrote.

The list of a dozen or more guests might include the chief executive officer of a corporation, a labor union official, a banker, a poet (Robert Frost), an artist, a lawyer, an airline president.

The invitations were for seven-thirty. I arrived at the White House alone and was escorted to an elevator to the family quarters on the second floor. The president received each of us in the yellow Oval Room, always a lovely reception room, but never as glittering as in the Eisenhower era. After the victory in the Second World War, each of the other Allied nations as well as the Russians presented a magnificent gift to the Supreme Allied Commander. All the gifts were swords decorated in different styles with precious stones, and these had been placed in separate glass cases around the perimeter of the East Room. Eisenhower walked with us commenting on each sword until he came to the Russian gift, a sword spectacularly encrusted with rubies, or so they appeared.

Since the treasures would eventually hang in the Eisenhower Presidential Library in Abilene, Kansas, his hometown, he had to have them insured. The insurance company balked at the jewels on the Russian sword. The agent maintained that the red stones were too pure to be genuine rubies, the president recounted. Both sides agreed to call a certain expert who was recognized as the foremost authority in America on rubies. Upon examination, he sided with the insurance company.

At eight o'clock, after drinks, the president escorted us to the State Dining Room on the first floor. One large round table accommodated all of us, and almost immediately the conversation was lively. At each of our places, incidentally, was a small penknife, a gift from our host. Soon a man across from me, a business executive, I believe, took a verbal swipe at Franklin D.

Roosevelt. I had a hunch that he was trying to please Eisenhower. If so, he failed. Eisenhower, to be sure, was no New Dealer. But he was quick to reply that Roosevelt's name was highly honored abroad, that it was an asset to the United States. Roosevelt was, undoubtedly, a great war leader, and who more than Eisenhower, when preparing in Great Britain for the Normandy invasion, would have been aware of it?

A gift from one ally to the victorious Supreme Commander could be seen only in Scotland, and in time, the president found it worth going to Scotland to enjoy it. The Scottish people presented him lifetime tenure in a sixteen-room apartment in Culzean (pronounced Cul-lanə) Castle, near Turnberry Point in the area of Prestwick. The castle was perched on a sheer cliff rising from the Firth of Clyde. Such a gift to Eisenhower, of course, required a golf course nearby. This one, only an overnight flight for Eisenhower's rich golfing partners in New York and Washington, had holes with such names as "Blaw Wearie," "Fin Me Oot," "Tappie Tourie," "Roon the Ben," "Dinna Fouter," "Tickley Tap," "Ca Canny," and "Lang Whang."

When Eisenhower, covered by the White House press, visited Europe in 1959, he put the castle on his itinerary with an earlier stop en route to spend a night as the guest of the queen at Balmoral Castle in Scotland. The route of our small motorcade carrying us there passed some beautiful homes with private driveways. As we approached Balmoral, the men who owned the houses stood at attention in their driveways. Their age made it look as though they might have been British officers under Eisenhower during the war. When his car passed, they snapped to attention and saluted him at *Present Arms*! It was a wonderful symbol that the salute was made, not with rifles, but with golf clubs.

Late in 1956, when Eisenhower's first term was drawing to an end, I wrote an article for *Collier's* about what the president would do in his second term. Without reference to the source, I drew on some things I had heard President Eisenhower say at the stag dinner. *Collier's* was delighted with the piece and planned to lead the inaugural issue in January with it. Only a few days later I got a call from the saddened *Collier's* Washington editor. The magazine was folding. *Collier's* office was only a few blocks from the National Press Building, and I hurried there and picked up the manuscript for my article. Then I grabbed a cab to the *Saturday Evening Post* bureau several blocks away. Almost on the spot, as I remember it, the *Post* gave me a $1,500 check. The article received a big play in a January issue under the headline "What Ike Will Do."

13

CHIEF OF THE *NEW YORK HERALD TRIBUNE* WASHINGTON BUREAU

By 1957, the *Herald Tribune* bureau in Washington was a mess long in the making. Bert Andrews, the chief in the 1940s and early 1950s, was a prizewinning star reporter with a Hearst background, a consuming relish for stories alleging postwar Communist espionage in America, and a deep attachment to Richard Nixon. Andrews, however, was a lone operator who took minimal interest in the workings of the bureau as a whole.

After his death in 1953, the Reids strangely replaced him with Roscoe Drummond of the *Christian Science Monitor*. Drummond was a fine, able man, but one who was detached from the style, customs, and lore of the *Herald Tribune*. He arrived at a time when there was a need for a chief who would become involved in the operations of the bureau. But he was like Andrews in the sense that his overwhelming interest was his own column. He recognized the problem. Indeed, he was eager to bring in someone who would be bureau chief in his own right. During the year I was on leave writing my book on Eisenhower, he tried. With heavy support from Brownie Reid, Don Whitehead of the Associated Press was hired. A splendid reporter who had won two Pulitzer Prizes as a war correspondent, he soon resigned because he did not like the job, or so he told me.

The unusual attention aroused by the Eisenhower book, combined with my years of experience with the *Herald Tribune* in New York and Washington, made me the likely choice, I suppose, to take over the bureau in 1956, and I was proud of it. I thought as much in terms of making over as taking over. It was not that the bureau lacked talent; but it had too few talented people to compete with the large, very experienced *New York Times* bureau.

We had a day desk man and a night desk man, but neither instilled professionalism. Essentially, they were copy handlers. I was able to make decided improvement with replacements. In 1958, I called George Cornish, the managing editor, and told him I was much impressed by the work of a reporter on the city staff, David Wise, whom I had never met. He had come to the *Tribune* in 1951 from Columbia College, where he had been editor of the *Spectator*, the student newspaper. I asked Cornish if we could have him. Wise came. He established himself as the best investigative reporter the bureau—probably the paper too, for that matter—ever had. In time, he was the White House correspondent, and eventually he succeeded me as bureau chief when I left in 1963. Over the years, he became a nationally recognized authority on espionage and the CIA and wrote several prominent books on the subject.

Another reporter whose work attracted me in 1958 was Warren Rogers Jr., who covered the State Department for the Associated Press. I called him just as he was considering an offer of a job at *Newsweek* in New York. He came to us as a military affairs reporter who could write well and fast. Our main political reporters were Earl Mazo, who had wide experience and acquaintances beyond Washington, and Rowland Evans Jr., who was on his way to becoming a syndicated columnist with Robert Novak. Evans focused on politics in Congress. Covering Capitol Hill was Don Irwin, a Princeton graduate and offspring of a literary family, who had recently been transferred from the city staff. Joseph Slevin, who had come from the *Journal of Commerce* and who published his own bond letter, joined us to write economic news, a field that had been a swamp in the old bureau. Robert C. Toth covered science and space. Tom Lambert, always dependable, who had been a foreign correspondent and would one day be assistant secretary of defense for public affairs, was now in the bureau. Also, for a time, was the rather notorious and very difficult Marguerite Higgins, who covered the State Department when it suited her purposes. I did not like having her in the bureau, but she was there, and her byline was of some value to the paper. Her exploits as a war correspondent in the Second World War and in Korea made her perhaps the best known woman reporter in the world.

The revitalized bureau had talent, verve, and an output that caught the eye. This change did not go unnoticed in Richard Kluger's book. Generously, he wrote that the bureau, since 1957, "had been rescued from turmoil and rebuilt into an alert, efficient news-gathering machine, better than at any other time in *Tribune* history."

Nevertheless, my hope for much-needed expansion was out of the question. The cramped Washington bureau was housed in one moderate-sized room with two small offices, one at each end. There was no library or timely clipping file. The place had room for a maximum of fifteen desks. No new talent could be accommodated. Moreover, since the paper had no retirement system to speak of, getting rid of older men whose best work was long behind them was practically inhuman. The bureau was isolated because there was no daily interchange of ideas with New York, except toward the very end during a last gasp of remaking the paper under John Denson, previously an editor of

Newsweek, and his two talented right-hand men, James G. Bellows and Richard C. Wald.

Maggie Higgins, as we all knew her, had joined the bureau while I was still on leave. The last time I had seen her was in late April of 1945, when the two of us were thrown out of the Overseas Writers Club for war correspondents in Paris. I had first met her in the *Herald Tribune* newsroom in New York before the war. In 1945, after the Second Division crossed the Rhine, I took my first furlough for three days in Paris. Never having been there before, when I got off the train I made my way to the Paris *Herald Tribune* building on the Rue de Berri at a time when Maggie, then a war correspondent, happened to be there. She invited me to have lunch with her the next day.

When we entered the rather splendid Overseas Writers Club, near the Opera, the sight of its crowded bar and the panorama of tablecloths and napkins was pure delight for one who had been living in the field for months. At our table we ordered drinks. Then the waiter brought the menus. Then appeared the very much agitated head waiter. "This is an officers' club," he told Maggie. "We cannot serve an enlisted man." Guess who belonged in that class? All foreign correspondents accredited to the European Theater of Operations held the assimilated rank of captain. Maggie was one of them, of course, and she replied with indignation suited to a captain. But words were useless.

Maggie and I finally had to rise and stamp out of the place. That I did not have the rank of captain, assimilated or otherwise, did not bother me in the least. What infuriated me was the sight of a bunch of correspondents from small-town papers in the United States huddled around the bar ordering one more while the *New York Herald Tribune* got the bum's rush.

It was a mistake for Maggie to persuade the executives in New York to send her to a bureau the size of ours in Washington. She was mercilessly ambitious and would make any kind of trouble to get her way. She was also likable, good-looking, and sexy. If she wanted somebody else's assignment, she would play any game to get it. In a large bureau like ours, however, it was harder for her to maneuver than when she was playing one-on-one. I followed the Bert Andrews policy of reserving the right to cover any story I chose, which, of course, included the biggest stories. Every other reporter in the bureau could write better than Maggie, and all of them knew how to defend their turfs. In large bureaus, traditions develop, traditions, for example, as to which stories the White House correspondent would cover or which the Pentagon reporter would take. This was a restraint on Maggie, who was at her best working on her own—a style that had helped her win one of six Pulitzer Prizes awarded for coverage of the Korean War.

Attempts to take the law into her own hands did not work for her either. Early in June 1960, when drama was building over the possibility that John F. Kennedy would be nominated for president at the Democratic National Convention in Los Angeles, Maggie let me know in midmonth that she expected to be included among our convention staff. I told her I could not agree to that. The reporters who regularly covered politics had a right to expect that they would go to the convention. Indeed, it was on their knowledge and contacts that we had to rely. When the convention began, for example, Earl Mazo learned that Governor-elect Terry Sanford would swing the North Carolina vote behind Kennedy. This would be the first break for Kennedy in the South, and the *Herald Tribune* had a clean beat on the story.

Maggie persisted, but another situation was developing that would require coverage of the State Department, her field. The rise of Fidel Castro to the dictatorship of Cuba infuriated President Eisenhower. He was shocked, among other things, by Castro's diatribes against the United States, by Castro's act of legalizing the Communist Party in Cuba, and by his seizure of some American-owned property on the island. Suddenly, the conflict sharpened. On July 6, 1960, Eisenhower issued an order virtually ending the sale of Cuban sugar in the United States. In reaction, on July 10, the Castro regime ruled that all American-owned companies in Cuba must record their resources to guide the decisions of the Cuban government in reacting to Eisenhower's action. I cautioned Maggie that she must stay close to the State Department on this. She might have the biggest story of us all. Then I left for Los Angeles.

The next day was the Saturday before the convention. We arranged our office in the Biltmore Hotel and filed a raft of stories to New York, leading with the near certainty of a Kennedy victory. At seven o'clock, Bobby Kennedy gave a reception for the press in the ballroom. When I entered, a sight that greeted me was Miss Marguerite Higgins holding forth in the middle of the room. I was less stunned than I might have been because I had been keeping an eye on the wire service news tickers for further developments in the Castro story, and there had been none of any consequence. Nominally, Saturday was Maggie's day off. She had paid all of her own travel expenses. Her presence did not win her any place in the paper's convention coverage. As I was to discover again before long, she had a compulsion to be in the center of prominent newspaper people on a big story, whether she was reporting that story or not.

In a matter of months, President Kennedy and Soviet Premier Nikita Khrushchev met in Vienna on June 3 and 4, 1961, at a time of gathering Soviet-American conflict over Berlin. The New York office was responsible for the coverage because the paper's various European bureaus were available. If the editors had wanted to send Maggie Higgins, that would have been agreeable to me, but they did not bring it up. My only responsibility was the assignment of a reporter to cover Kennedy. That reporter would inevitably do the lead story out of Vienna because he would be in close touch with the White House staff. I assigned David Wise, then the White House correspondent, and Maggie was furious. I felt sorry for her. But it was traditional for the White House reporter to cover presidential trips. Furthermore, Wise would write a much better running story on the Kennedy-Khrushchev meeting than Maggie would have. I doubtless would have gone to Vienna, too, but my vacation was to begin the next day. It was to consist of four weeks of digging into the story of the PT (patrol, torpedo) boats skippered by John F. Kennedy during the war in the Pacific. The search for details about *PT 109* and *PT 59* would take me to Australia, the Solomon Islands, and Japan.

A month later, on my return to Washington, I learned that Maggie had turned up in Vienna, ostensibly on an assignment from some magazine. The situation was lamentable.

For her, the future held happiness and tragedy. She and I were still friends when she left the *Herald Tribune* and went with *Newsday* as a syndicated columnist. She was married to a splendid man, Air Force General William Hall, and they had two daughters. She went to Vietnam to cover the war there and contracted a fatal tropical disease, from which she died in 1966 at the age of forty-five. As the wife of General Hall, she was buried in Arlington National Cemetery.

14

TWENTIETH-CENTURY ODYSSEY
PRESIDENT EISENHOWER'S MEGATRIP TO ASIA AND INDIA

During Dwight Eisenhower's years in office, two changes drastically altered the nature of the presidency. One was the advent of television, which revolutionized American politics. The other was the coming of the jet passenger plane. President Roosevelt had the *Sacred Cow* and Truman the *Independence*, but both were propeller planes. Long trips in either of them would be slow in comparison with what was possible in a jet. In his first year in office, Eisenhower had a propeller plane, the *Columbine II*. Then in the summer of 1959, new scope was added to the presidency when he received a four-engine Boeing 707 jet. It was designated *Air Force One*, as have been all presidential jets ever since. The jet enabled Eisenhower and his successors to project themselves and their influence into countries around the globe. Theretofore, practical considerations limited how far a president could travel abroad and how long he could stay away. With the jet, no place was more than hours from Washington in case of an emergency. When Eisenhower received *Air Force One* in 1959, he had invitations from heads of state in India and several Asian countries. He was delighted with the prospect of a historical international tour, and he and his party departed Washington on December 3, 1959. The reporters assigned to cover him traveled in a chartered commercial jet plane.

As an indication of his high spirits, Eisenhower gave an unusual cocktail party the night before in the State Dining Room in the White House for the reporters and officials who would accompany him. The itinerary called for him to travel 22,370 miles to visit eleven nations on three continents. No president of the United States had ever before seen, or been seen by, such masses of people. As he neared the end of his journey in Morocco, large crowds gathered to get a look at the American "sultan." Some of the scenes en route in India and Asia evidently conveyed the image of a ruler of an empire, although nothing like it was intended by the traveler.

Rome was the first stop, and the day was spoiled by ceaseless heavy rain. Eisenhower was welcomed at the airport by Giovanni Gronchi, the president of Italy.

"The ride in was fabulous on the old Appian Way," Eisenhower's confidential secretary, Ann Whitman, noted in her diary. "The road was lined with what I guess were tombs of Caesar's soldiers.... Later I saw parts of the old Roman wall.... What beats me is how they have adjusted the modern age to the antiquities about them—traffic weaving beneath the old Roman wall, for instance."

The weather squelched the prospect of large crowds, but small groups dotted the route, and the president heard for the first time on the trip chants of "Viva Ike." I dare say, before he returned home, he heard the equivalent in many other languages from millions of voices.

Eisenhower was a guest at the four-hundred-year-old stately Quirinal Palace, which stands on one of the seven hills of Rome and is the official residence of Rome's presidents. The ceiling of his bedroom was painted with religious imagery.

The next day he had a private audience with Pope John XXIII, which made him only the second American president to have had such an engagement. The *Star-Spangled Banner* was heard in a Vatican courtyard for the first time since January 4, 1919, when President Woodrow Wilson was received by Pope Benedict XV. Before his talk with President Eisenhower, however, John XXIII decided to meet with the traveling reporters. I was fascinated, never having seen a pope. I hope no reader will be offended if I recall that when he entered, I whispered to a colleague, "My God, he looks like Mayor La Guardia." The mayor, it will be recalled, was of Italian descent. The two men seemed to me to have similar builds.

In a short talk, the pope bade us never to betray the truth. "Truth," he said, "is the most precious thing of all." He ventured that if Saint Paul, one of the early Christians, were alive in 1959, he would be a journalist. If so, Paul might be amazed at what reporters go through writing and filing copy on the run during 22,370 miles of often feverish travel with a president in a jet plane.

The spectacle that rain had prevented in Rome burst forth the next day in Ankara, Turkey. Ankara, we were told, had been built since the First World War and had a population of more than five hundred thousand. Every single resident of this capital of Turkey appeared to have turned out to acclaim the president of the United States.

"Turks Are Your Real Friends, Ike," read a large banner. On entering the city, his car was stopped while a folk dance of welcome was performed by a group of men called Zeybecks, who were dressed in peasant costumes and wore bandannas.

The presidential motorcade rolled through three miles of streets behind mounted lancers. Along the way were respected janissary bands. Janissaries, it was explained to us, were guards of the sultans in the days of the Ottoman Empire. Thousands of people danced in the streets, wearing bright costumes, cheering, waving flags, and shouting, "Yasha" ("Long Life"). On occasion, after Eisenhower's car had passed, spectators ran after him. Wasn't it unusual for people to run after a foreign visitor? What did it signify? What did they know about a president that would arouse them? Were the crowds sophisticated enough to view Eisenhower as the man perhaps most likely to preserve peace? Whatever the reason, he was a magnet to crowds in every country he visited. One spectator in Ankara brandished a sign reading, "Welcome Aix." This was hardly up to "Ike," but still better than "Ick." Ankara University did the best, with a color portrait of Eisenhower painted by students and hanging six stories tall on one of the university's buildings.

At dusk, the president drove out for a wreath-laying ceremony at what was considered the most sacred spot in Turkey, the tomb of Kemal Atatürk, the founder of modern Turkey, who died in 1938. The vast sand-colored marble edifice with large columns crowned a hill overlooking Ankara. By the time we reached the tomb, it was dark and cold. Wind blew through the columns. The lighting was dim. I could not remember a bleaker scene.

That night in Ankara, Eisenhower was honored at a dinner in the presidential residence. The menu was Turkish caviar, American soup, sea bass sauteed with shrimp sauce, roast beef, salad, Turkish pastry with crème, fruit, and coffee. The wines were Cankaya, Yildiz Danlafi 1952, and champagne, which should have been enough to brace President Eisenhower for a very strenuous visit to Karachi, Pakistan, the next day, December 8.

All along the way in Asia we glimpsed the contrast between a certain splendor and the prevalent squalor. In Karachi, against the glitter of Eisenhower's triumphant procession, I could see scores of human eyes peering out through openings in mud huts. Eisenhower unquestionably saw life-size tableaux of the problems in Asia that increasingly occupied the attention of government officials in Washington. In the outskirts of Karachi, the president passed through a marsh so malodorous it had been sprayed earlier to reduce the stench. In addition to military aid, the United States was then spending about $250 million a year in various forms of economic assistance to Pakistan. It was probably in reference to that that signs along Eisenhower's route read "Thank You America."

In speaking to a large crowd at a polo ground, he promised that the United States would continue to help Pakistan raise its standard of living.

He offered hope that some day nuclear energy could be harnessed to benefit this underdeveloped part of the world.

That was for the future. The scenes of Eisenhower's visit were spectacular. Estimates of a turnout of a million persons may well have been accurate. Crowds were so dense that at one point I could hear a band playing nearby, yet could not see it. The president first rode in an automobile, then changed to a horse-drawn coach behind a squadron of red-clad lancers. No "Viva Ike." The Pakistanis cried "Zindabad Ike." Zindabad means "long life" in Urdu.

The most common dress for men and women seemed to be loose-fitting white pajamas underneath rather long coats. With the temperature at eighty-five degrees, most people wore sandals, although the obviously poor were barefoot. Some women wore veils with only a narrow aperture at the eyes. Others wore beautiful silk saris of a lemon color or lavender or pink. Some were dressed in "dopattas," an open-face veil that hung all the way to the feet. Some men wore fezzes or the Punjabi headdress or a kind of turban familiar to people of the region of the Khyber Pass. Stores along the way were strung with electric lights.

Then, of course, there were the snake charmers in turbans. At one square Eisenhower passed, he was feted by a man playing a flutelike instrument called in Ankara a *bansri*, to which an undulating cobra was doing what was immediately dubbed in the press bus as the latest Pakistani "rock 'n' roll."

Russ Baker was certainly not a boaster, yet we all seemed to know that he had been a great high hurdler in high school. Before that day in Karachi passed, none of us doubted it. While he was walking along a sidewalk, a man sidled up to him peddling his wares in a large burlap bag. When a glimpse revealed that the merchandise was a mass of writhing snakes, Baker crossed a main thoroughfare in about six bounds.

That day President Eisenhower laid a wreath on the tomb of Mohammed Ali Jinnah, the founder of Pakistan. Customs required that anyone who approached the tomb must either remove his shoes or cover them. Eisenhower covered his shoes with white canvas boots.

Flying next from Pakistan to Afghanistan brought us so deeply into central Asia that it was puzzling at first why an American president would choose to visit Afghanistan. Still, Afghanistan bordered on the Soviet Union, and signs of Soviet influence would attract our attention. In fact, Soviet-built MiG fighters with Afghan pilots escorted *Air Force One* on the approach to Bagram Airport, built by Soviets. From there it was almost an hour's drive to Kabul, the capital. Stepping off the plane, I had never felt so isolated, and I wondered if the president had any such feeling. Glancing around, it looked as if time had been turned back a thousand years. The airport stood in a vast hollow surrounded by the distant, towering, snow-covered Hindu Kush mountains. The weather was cold. The road to Kabul, thirty-eight miles to the north, was narrow. It would have been sensible, if not acceptable, for the reporters to refuse to board the press bus of Soviet manufacture. The ride ahead was terrifying.

We could tell from the start that the bus was a very loose-steering vehicle. It had to be an instinct for survival that caused the driver to turn the wheel at the last possible moment to keep from going over embankments. Most horrifying were his spurts through numerous villages. On either side, the houses and other buildings came down almost to the edge of the narrow road. In every village, crowds had squeezed out to watch the Eisenhower motorcade pass. Each time, as it became obvious that the driver was not going to slow down, we covered our eyes for fear of seeing men, women, and children mangled. Brakes were never used when coming into villages. Salvation lay in liberal use of the horn.

In the isolated city of Kabul, the president's only appointment was with the khaki-clad King Mohammad Zahir Shah at the nearby Chilistoon Palace. Meanwhile, several of us reporters descended on White House Press Secretary James C. Hagerty and pressed him to get us another driver for the return to the airport. To good effect, he did.

Now we took off for the flight over the renowned Khyber Pass and on to India, always the goal of Eisenhower's odyssey. He arrived at Palam Airport in New Delhi after dark on December 10, 1959. A glimpse of the waiting multitude, it was said, made it seem as though the morning rush-hour crowd at Fifth Avenue and Forty-second Street in New York ran into the evening rush-hour crowd just as the St. Patrick's Day Parade was passing through. Nevertheless, it was not the size of the crowd that counted, but its dynamic. It gave me the lead for my story to the *New York Herald Tribune*: "India exploded in a welcome to President Eisenhower tonight."

He was the first American president to visit India, and the scene quickly became frightening. As we tried to get into the press bus, teenage Indians struggled to push their way in with us. When we kept them out, they attempted to climb in through the windows only to find them barred. Then, what really seemed dangerous, especially in the warm weather, was that they scrambled up on the roof of the bus. How many could the roof hold without caving in, leaving a stifled mass of youths and reporters with no way for anyone to reach a door?

The motorcade was engulfed in a mass of yelling, shoving men, a serious problem for the Secret Service, which was responsible for the president's safety. In fact, Indian Prime Minister Jawaharlal Nehru jumped out of the car in which he was seated with Eisenhower and strove without success to flail the mob away. The car in which Ann Whitman and Colonel Andrew J. Goodpaster were riding was almost overflowing with tossed flowers. In spite of the darkness, both of them put on sunglasses to protect their eyes from cascades of marigolds. Eventually, the police were able to detach the president's car from the motorcade and rush him to the Rashtrapati Bhavan, an official residence. Once refreshed in his suite, he glowed over his reception, according to Mrs. Whitman. He invited his staff for drinks and dinner on that same day that they had eaten breakfast in Pakistan and lunch in Afghanistan. The next morning they were awakened by a band playing in the courtyard.

During the week, Eisenhower addressed Parliament and later joined Nehru in addressing a huge outdoor gathering. The two leaders had met earlier in Washington. The president then remarked to Ann Whitman that Nehru "was wholly unaware of our general trend of thinking, just as we may be unaware of their thinking."

The president's visit to India would end the following Sunday in Agra, where he would take a long-desired look at the white marble Taj Mahal. The *New York Times* bureau in New Delhi had a car, and Russ Baker managed to borrow it and its native driver so that he, Peter Lisagor (then of the *Chicago Daily News*), and I could go on ahead and glimpse the Indian landscape and then view the Taj Mahal at night. The ride was pleasant, and the Taj Mahal a sight of ceaseless beauty rising out of a walled garden. We had rooms in a hotel in Agra and finished the night in a barnlike barroom downstairs.

We knew we would have to check out early the next morning because it was imperative for us to rejoin the Eisenhower entourage in downtown Agra. In the crowds that the president was sure to draw, we could never make it to the airport by ourselves in the car. We had to board the press bus in Agra. With our driver, we rolled away from the hotel for a couple of blocks. After that, we found ourselves in a massive traffic jam. In all directions, carts drawn by bullocks lumbered about. Old automobiles, hundreds of bicycles, farm wagons, and pedestrians by the hundred were all creeping toward the Taj Mahal. Then came a ghastly interlude. I was sitting in the back seat of the car. Baker was in the front next to the driver. Suddenly emerging from the crowd, a wild-looking man in a turban and flapping clothes pushed straight to the right side of our car, where the front window was down.

High in his left hand he held the throat of a huge snake, a python, I supposed. His right hand dragged the body of the reptile, the long tail of which disappeared in the crowd. What was the wild man up to? Was he just bringing a prize to show us? Could he have imagined that we would buy it? "Close the window!" I hollered. Baker spun it up just in time against the big face of the snake. If the window had not been closed as fast as it was, the wild man might have been able to shove the whole snake inside the car on top of Baker, the driver, and me. It is much pleasanter to recall that even as we escaped this fright, we caught sight of our press bus, and our driver let us off as near as he could get to it.

President Eisenhower's principal visits were now behind him, but the road back to Washington was still a long one. After taking off from New Delhi following the visit to the Taj Mahal, he made it all the way to Athens by nightfall, with a stop en route in Tehran to call on Shah Mohammad Reza Pahlavi. Along the road from Mehrabad Airport to the royal palace, we were greeted by a succession of bands, practically all of them playing "The Colonel Bogie March," which had recently been popularized in the movie *The Bridge on the River Kwai*. Of all the symbols of welcoming we had seen since the beginning of our tour in Rome, nothing exceeded Tehran's. For at least a mile on the thoroughfare leading to the shah's palace from the airport, the road was covered with Persian rugs. When I glanced down from an open window of the heavy bus and watched its wheels rolling over them, I wondered if we were guilty of vandalism. At a luncheon in the palace, Ann Whitman was told the buses were good for the carpets.

In Athens, we had time to visit the magnificent scene of the Parthenon before leaving for Tunisia. From there, we traveled on to France. In Paris, the president had talks with British Prime Minister Harold Macmillan, General Charles de Gaulle of France, and the West German chancellor, Konrad Adenauer. On December 22, the last day of the trip, the president had breakfast in the Prado Palace in Madrid with Generalissimo Francisco Franco. After that he flew to Casablanca to talk with King Mohamad V of Morocco. It was a rifle-bearing Berber tribesman who said he had come to see the "sultan of America."

On the pre-Christmas return to the United States, no memorable pronouncements were made unless it was the statement of the speechwriter Kevin McCann, who said: "I don't know how many friends we made . . . for the United States; in fact, we may have lost a few. But, by God, we kept the schedule!"

I felt that Eisenhower's odyssey was worthwhile. It was obvious that his visits aroused goodwill, even if they were of passing significance. He broached no new programs, no change in policy. In essence, Eisenhower's trip was one of self-fulfillment, a worthy statesman's dream. Already, December 1959 was late in his second term. In several months, the Democratic and Republican national conventions would meet and nominate John Kennedy and Richard Nixon, respectively, one of whom—Kennedy—would succeed Eisenhower. Nixon would enter the White House later. Thereupon, he topped Eisenhower a bit by taking a presidential trip completely around the world. I covered it for the *Los Angeles Times*, but Nixon's odyssey was no match for the spectacle of Eisenhower's, except for the presence of Pat Nixon's charming press secretary.

15

Things I Learned under the Capitol Dome

After publication of my Eisenhower book, I received a telephone call from Robert Cousins of McGraw-Hill Books, offering me $10,000 to do an as-told-to book with Joseph W. Martin Jr. (that is, Martin's story as told to Donovan). Martin had twice been speaker of the House of Representatives. As early as 1916, he was a Massachusetts delegate to the Republican National Convention in Chicago, where he voted for the nomination of Charles Evans Hughes, who was defeated in the election by Woodrow Wilson. In time, Martin was to become the permanent chairman of five other Republican conventions. On three occasions he himself was a dark-horse contender for the nomination. "Each time," he told me later, "the white horses were too numerous and swift." He was the campaign manager for Wendell L. Willkie of Indiana in his turbulent but losing campaign against Franklin D. Roosevelt in 1940. Since 1939, Joe had been the Republican floor leader in the House. At the time I came into the picture, however, he had just been unseated by the younger Representative Charles A. Halleck, also of Indiana.

Martin retained his hideaway, a good-sized office directly under the rim of the Capitol dome, and that is where we worked each morning. To me the project offered a wonderful glimpse of a fading politician of national importance and integrity whose like we shall not encounter again.

"As a boy in North Attleboro, Massachusetts, where I was born and still live," he told me, "I listened to Jacob S. Coxey recruiting his 'army' of unemployed for the descent on Washington after the Panic of 1893. In 1896, I marched in a torchlight parade for William McKinley. When I became a politician in my own right, I campaigned in 1911, transported by horse and buggy or interurban. In those day, politicians seldom had automobiles. A nickel got me to Seekonk on the trolley in ample time to address a meeting." In those days there was no problem with campaign funds, hard or soft.

"I served in the Massachusetts legislature with Calvin Coolidge; a close bond developed between us that endured throughout his years in the White House," Martin recalled.

In Washington one evening, he dined with the Coolidges in the Willard Hotel and then visited with them in their suite. Coolidge asked his wife to get his golf clubs. "These sticks are a little dirty, Grace," the future president said, with what Joe thought was an air of suggestion that she should have kept them clean.

What was new to Joe at the 1924 convention in Cleveland was that it was the first one broadcast by radio. John Philip Sousa led the band in "The Stars and Stripes Forever." During lulls in the program, people sang "The Long, Long Trail." One practice then that mercifully has not carried over into the present was the eagerness of some orators to set parts of their speeches to rhyme.

Representative Theodore Elijah Burton of Ohio drew applause when he intoned:

> *Oh, that there might 'mongst*
> *Propagandists be*
> *A duty on hypocrisy,*
> *A tax on humbug*
> *An impost on dreary platitudes*
> *A stamp athwart the mouth*
> *Of everyone that ranted*

The gavel was in Martin's hand on the podium in Philadelphia in 1940, during one of the most uproarious Republican conventions of the twentieth century. The leading contenders were Wendell Willkie, Senator Robert A. Taft of Ohio, and Tom Dewey of New York. As the convention moved toward the fifth ballot, the hall was in pandemonium, dominated by massive chants of "We Want Willkie!" Trying to restore order, Martin said, "If you'll wait awhile, maybe you'll get him."

On the fifth ballot Kansas swung its eighteen votes to Willkie, flinging the convention into such upheaval that Martin could barely control it. While vacationing in Buffalo, I listened to the convention on the radio at the Saturn Club, where the excitement among members and guests almost matched that in Philadelphia.

When the roll call reached North Dakota, a delegate responded: "North Dakota casts four votes for Senator Taft and four votes for Vendell Villkie."

"For who?" Martin demanded.

"For Vendell Villkie," the delegate repeated.

"Spell it," Martin ordered.

The thunder of laughter in the hall eased the convention through a very tense moment. On the sixth ballot Willkie was nominated.

When Eisenhower was president, he found it difficult, according to his biographer, Stephen E. Ambrose, to work effectively with Martin as House minority leader. Eisenhower characterized Martin as a "courageous fighter," Ambrose noted, but complained that "it was almost impossible to get him to understand any subtle suggestions."

Martin was an encyclopedia on political speeches. He recalled a day in the House where an aroused Democrat got himself so engulfed in clichés that he practically shouted, "I say to you, Mr. Speaker, that politics make strange bedfellows. Especially since women got into 'em." In fact, Joe told me that after thirty-five years in Congress, he had heard almost every kind of speaker the nation had produced.

"We used to call Representative James O'Connor of Louisiana the sunset speaker," he said, "because he made a speech in the House every day at sunset. And Representative William I. Sirovich of New York was the B.C. [before Christ] speaker. A physician who wrote several plays that were produced on Broadway, Sirovich set his speeches in a framework that went back centuries before Christ. When I first heard him, he was back around 500 B.C. I used to ask him, 'Can't you get us up to date a little faster?' But I do not think that during his years in Congress he ever progressed much beyond A.D. 100 as his starting point."

During the administration of President Herbert Hoover, it chanced that there was a redistricting of Massachusetts. A seat that was squeezed out was that of Republican Representative Frederick W. Dallinger, who was much liked by his colleagues. Two of them, Representatives Edith Nourse Rogers and Joe Martin, were appointed by the state's delegation to call on the president and ask him to appoint Dallinger judge of the United State Customs Court. Hoover liked Dallinger and agreed to do it. When Mrs. Rogers rose to thank him, she tripped over a wire, yanking the telephone off Hoover's desk.

"That's the way with a woman, Mr. President," Martin said. "Give her a judgeship, and she wants the telephone, too."

▲ Donovan and other reporters chat with President Truman's daughter, Margaret, aboard the Truman campaign train as it neared Kansas City in 1949.

This chat between President Kennedy and Donovan in the Oval Office in 1961 doubtless bore on Donovan's work on a book about the drama of Kennedy's experiences as a PT boat commander in the war with Japan. ▼

◀ Whoever it was who caught Donovan's attention on the telephone in the old White House press room, it was not President Eisenhower.

Donovan shows Kennedy photos of the Pacific island on which Kennedy and his PT boat crew took refuge when their boat was sunk by a Japanese destroyer. ▼

▲ In the White House the president receives Benjamin Kevu, one of the natives who rescued him and his crew while they were hiding from the Japanese on a deserted island. Watching Kennedy and his guest are George "Barney" Ross, a member of the crew on the night of the collision, and Donovan.

President Johnson introduces Donovan to a White House visitor. ▼

▲ Donovan, in the dark coat, takes notes while covering President Nixon's visit to the Berlin Wall on February 27, 1969.

Donovan listens as President Ford relates the immediate problems facing him as he takes over the White House following the resignation of President Nixon. ▼

▲ Donovan addresses a joint meeting of Congress in honor of the hundredth anniversary of President Truman's birth in 1884.

▼ Margaret Truman introduces Donovan to President Reagan in the White House.

▲ In his earliest days in office in 1993, President Clinton talks with two *Los Angeles Times* reporters, Jack Nelson and Robert Donovan.

16

Score One for Jock Whitney

In peacetime, certainly, it would be very unusual for a large, competitive newspaper to kill, at the last moment, a major story exclusively in its possession. That happened at the *Herald Tribune* during the first week of the Kennedy administration. David Wise, Warren Rogers Jr., and I, all members of the Washington bureau, urged the dropping of a story we ourselves had uncovered, and Fendall Yerxa, the managing editor, supported us.

On the evening of January 24, 1961, four days after the Kennedy inaugural, I attended the annual informal Gridiron Club dinner held to discuss the nature of the skits we would put on at the large white-tie dinner in the spring. Seated next to me was one of my best friends among Washington reporters, Arthur Sylvester, formerly of the *Newark News*. He retained associate membership in the club, although he had dropped out of newspaper work to join the new administration as an assistant to Secretary of Defense Robert S. McNamara. When we settled down, Sylvester said to me, "I suppose you will be downtown at 1 A.M. tonight?"

On the contrary, I had every intention of going home when the dinner was over. What would I be doing downtown at 1 A.M.? The table came alive with conversation, but I could not shake off Sylvester's reference to 1 A.M. No doubt one reason was that I could not forget that at 1 A.M. on April 11, 1951, reporters at the White House were handed copies of a statement that President Truman had fired General MacArthur. My family and I had moved to another house the day before, and neither the *Herald Tribune* bureau nor the White House press office had our new telephone number yet. I knew nothing about the MacArthur drama until I picked up the *Washington Post* on the front steps the next morning. Because of that experience, Arthur Sylvester's remark at dinner would not die. When we were putting on our coats to leave later, he murmured to me that he was sure I was not going home.

I went to the National Press Building, reopened the bureau, and called up Wise, our White House correspondent, and Rogers, our military affairs correspondent. Neither of them had heard about a one o'clock announcement, and both started telephoning. Because Rogers was familiar with an array of Pentagon problems, he recalled an event of July 1, 1960. A U.S. Air Force RB-47 reconnaissance plane with a crew of six, while flying from Great

Britain on an electronic intelligence mission, had been shot down by the Soviets over the Barents Sea, north of Norway and Russia. Only two members of the crew lived to parachute to safety, and they were imprisoned by the Russians. Could it be that these fliers were about to be released now? In a telephone conversation with a source in the Pentagon, Rogers pretended to know all about it, whereupon the source, off the record, innocently confirmed his speculation.

We called Yerxa and told him that the White House was going to break a big story at 1 A.M. He stopped the presses in New York so the story could be carried in most copies of the Late City Edition, the large run.

Meanwhile, Wise had reached Pierre Salinger at home. When the president's press secretary learned what we were up to, he "sputtered," Wise recalled later, "like a Roman candle in a light rain." Salinger made no attempt to deny our story but argued that advance publication would be hostile to national security. The two Americans were still in Soviet hands. An agreement had been reached with the Russians for simultaneous announcement of their release. Premature disclosure, Salinger warned, could kill the deal, prolonging the fliers' imprisonment. In still another call, Salinger told Wise he was speaking on behalf of President Kennedy in appealing to us not to run the story.

Wise called me to report this. He said it was a difficult decision, but he thought that under the circumstances we ought not to file a story. If publication upset the agreement and kept the fliers in prison, the *Herald Tribune* would be blamed. The risk was too big to take. If David Wise, of all people, favored killing a good exclusive news story, who could oppose it? We had to delay publication or endanger the future of two American fliers. I called Yerxa, and the Late City Edition resumed its run. At the same time, the 1 A.M. deadline lost its meaning. In Moscow, a KLM flight with the American fliers aboard blew a tire while preparing for takeoff, and it was 5 P.M. Eastern Standard Time the next day before they were in the air. At a televised press conference an hour later, the president happily announced that the fliers were on their way home, and the Kremlin was making a similar statement.

An incident like this was not the sort of affair in which a newspaper publisher, especially the charming, very Republican publisher of the *Herald Tribune*, John Hay Whitney, was apt to be involved. It is doubtful that he knew anything of the deliberations over the 1 A.M. deadline. The day after Kennedy's press conference, however, Whitney found himself praised at the direction of the new Democratic president. Kennedy instructed Salinger to send Whitney a telegram commending the paper for holding up the story of the fliers. The telegram said that the Whitney newspaper had prevented the violation of an agreement between the United States and the Soviet Union over announcement of the fliers' release. Needless to say, the telegram made an excellent front-page story in the *Herald Tribune*. Privately my own praise was showered, without his knowing it, on Arthur Sylvester.

17

Chronicling John Kennedy's Close Calls on *PT 109* and *PT 59*

The Martin book was published at the start of the 1960 presidential campaign. At the approach of the Kennedy inauguration, I got a call from Ed Kuhn, editor of the trade book department of McGraw-Hill, asking me if I would try my hand at a book about Kennedy's adventures as skipper of *PT 109* in the South Pacific during the war against Japan. While I would not have wished to get involved in a political book about Kennedy, I liked Kuhn's idea. Working on a book such as he had mentioned could bring me, the bureau chief of a Republican newspaper, a particular entrée to the new president. I told Kuhn I knew Kennedy. I had covered much of his 1960 campaign and was sure I could solicit his help on the book.

Unquestionably, Kennedy's reputation as a war hero had helped him win the election. After the war the author John Hersey had written an article entitled "Survival," which was published in the *New Yorker*. In the article, Hersey described how the ship commanded by Ambassador Kennedy's son had been wrecked in a collision with a Japanese destroyer and the young Kennedy had gallantly helped rescue most of his crew.

With inaugural festivities in Washington already swirling, I would have to wait until late January to talk to the new president. From my own experiences in the infantry, I knew that it was common for episodes to be recounted as being more exalted than they in fact were. Before undertaking a war book, ought I not satisfy myself that the subject was as it was hailed? Was there any unknown aspect of the ramming of *PT 109* and the aftermath that, if disclosed, would shed a different light on the episode? Who could tell me? Who, for example, was certain to have heard through naval sources about any act or circumstances that had not come to light?

There was precisely such a person. He was Admiral Arleigh Burke, chief of naval operations and a member of the Joint Chiefs of Staff. In the war, ships under his command were in action the same night as Kennedy's boat was shipwrecked and in waters not far removed.

I had worked hard to cultivate the admiral as a news source. Indeed, one year he invited my late wife and me to ride in his special car on the train to an Army-Navy game. Admiral Burke had flourished in the Eisenhower administration, but rumors at the Pentagon had it that he was rather at odds with Senator Kennedy. After I heard from Ed Kuhn, I made an appointment with Admiral Burke. In his office at the Pentagon I explained why I had to be circumspect in a book on *PT 109*. He understood me. He swung to the right in his chair and looked out the window. Then he swung back and said, "On that, Kennedy was all right."

A couple of days after the 1961 inauguration, I was seated by President Kennedy's desk. Through Pierre Salinger, the president knew I was eager to write a book on his dramatic wartime experiences in the South Pacific in 1943.

"Oh, Bob," Kennedy said to me, "don't get into that. You'll be flogging a dead horse."

Referring to Hersey's article, he continued:

"Every time I ran for office after the war, we made a million copies of that article to throw around. There is really nothing more for you to tell."

I could not let that stand.

"If Ambassador Kennedy's son, the now-sitting president of the United States, was a naval officer whose boat was rammed by the Japanese in the war, leaving him shipwrecked in the South Seas," I said, "there would be a lot more to tell about it than can be covered in an article a few thousand words long."

I strove to avoid disappointing Ed Kuhn after he had come to me with the idea.

"We are now at that point, Mr. President," I went on, "where every phase of a president's career becomes the subject for a separate book. A book like this would be in libraries and archives. Future readers might never come upon the Hersey article in old magazines."

While I was still at the president's desk, Ted Reardon, a delightful member of Kennedy's staff, came into the room and overheard some of the conversation.

"Ted," the president interposed, "tell the navy to make anything they have on this subject available to Bob." Then he turned to me and said, "So go ahead and work on it, if that is what you want to do. If you still think you have a book, come back and I'll help you if I can."

So much about this tale is ironic. When it became certain that my nearly completed book would be published, I reminded the president through Salinger of his promise of help. On July 5, 1961, the three of us had lunch together in the family quarters of the White House. Try as I might, I could barely get a word out of Kennedy on his ordeals in the Solomons. He was so anxious about his recent difficult meeting with Nikita Khrushchev in

Vienna—the one that led to the erection of the Berlin Wall—that he was not interested in talking about anything else. He did not specify that what he was saying was off the record. Obviously, it would make a good news story, and to report such stories is what the *Herald Tribune* kept me in Washington for. After lunch, I went back to the bureau and wrote that story. The next morning, the *Trib* led the paper with it under the headline, "Highest View: Berlin Crisis Short of War."

I braced myself for a testy call from Salinger, but the phone did not ring. In retrospect, maybe Kennedy said what he did on a hunch that I would publish it. The gist of his words lessened public anxiety about a possible Soviet-American clash over Berlin.

Kennedy did make one resounding comment about *PT 109* at that lunch. "That affair," he said, "was more fucked up than Cuba." The reference, of course, was to the Bay of Pigs disaster in Cuba on April 17, 1961. That day, a force of fourteen hundred anti-Castro Cuban exiles, organized, trained, transported, and directed by the United States, was crushed during an attempted landing in Cuba without air support. The undertaking, aimed at expelling Castro, had its origins in the Eisenhower administration but was, to his own great embarrassment, approved in the end by President Kennedy.

Word had spread through the Press Building that I was writing a book on Kennedy's exploits in the Solomon Islands. A colleague of mine, Patrick Munroe, sauntered into my office one evening and told me he was interested in PT boats. In fact, I learned that he as well as Kennedy had been a PT boat skipper, and the two were good friends in the islands. Pat flabbergasted me by saying that he had some money and would like to invest as much as $50,000 in my book. I had no idea how much money I might make on the Kennedy project. Warmly as I like Pat Munroe and his wife, Mary, I felt that this was a book that was very personal with me and that no one else should have a hand in it. As things turned out, I would have lost what would have been a small fortune in my eyes by splitting the income from that book with anybody, although working with Pat would have been a delight.

The wartime relationship between Munroe and Kennedy was fascinating. In the South Pacific in 1943, Lieutenant Patrick Munroe was skipper of *PT 110*. In preparation for an offensive, the navy wanted six of the boats sent to New Guinea. After five had been assigned, Munroe and Kennedy agreed to flip a coin to determine which would go to New Guinea and which to the Solomons. Munroe tossed up a fifty-cent piece and told Kennedy, "Call it." "Tails." "Heads it is," Munroe said, and prepared to depart for New Guinea, which was his preference. Thereupon, Kennedy headed to the Solomons and, for all anyone knew, to the White House.

Beginning immediately after my first talk with the president, I devoted every Saturday for the next couple of months to travel to interview surviving members of Kennedy's *PT 109* crew. The men were scattered from Massachusetts to California, from Florida to Illinois. With names like McMahon, Harris, Johnston, Starkey, Drawdy, Kowal, Ross, Drewitch, Mauer, Zinzer, and Maguire, they were intelligent workingmen, mostly. Harold Mamey and Andrew Jackson Kirksey disappeared in the crash. Survivors regarded their disastrous collision with the Japanese destroyer *Amagiri* ("Heavenly Mist") as the most dramatic event of their lives. The *Amagiri* was one of a flotilla of four Japanese destroyers that had swept south through the islands on a supply mission. When their task was completed they headed back north and were spotted by American outposts. *PT 109* and three companion boats based on the island of Rendova were ordered into Blackett Strait, the size of a lake, to confront and torpedo them. In a night as black as tar, the *Amagiri*, under the command of Captain Kohei Hanami, was running at thirty knots, almost exactly in the direction of the waiting *PT 109*. Hanami and Kennedy sighted each other at about the same time. It was shortly after midnight on August 2, 1943.

"Hard a-starboard," Captain Hanami called.

"General quarters," Kennedy ordered.

All the surviving members told me essentially the same story with altogether a profusion of fresh detail. While these interviews carried me a long way, they also left gaps. Different crew members, for example, remembered the sequences of events differently, which tortured narrative. None knew the names of the three islands, one after another, on which they found safety. On this score, the navy's maps were of no help. From what the survivors told me, all of the crew admired and, in some cases, revered Kennedy for his skill and his leadership in their rescue and in averting their capture and death at the hands of the Japanese. The most conspicuous rescue was that of Patrick McMahon, who emerged from the fiery crash with massive burns. Kennedy, who had been a member of the Harvard swimming team, turned McMahon over on his back in the water. One end of the strap on McMahon's kapok jacket had been cut by Kennedy and was floating loose. Kennedy clamped it in his teeth and for hours, almost to the point of exhaustion, towed McMahon through the water for perhaps three or four miles.

This is not the place to retell the story of *PT 109*. It is an opportunity to recall how the story (some critics referred to it approvingly as a documentary) was put together eighteen years after the event. While talks with the crew were essential, a very good war story could not be told adequately through the interviews. I did not even have a clear picture of the scene, which sometime later I found described in the lines of Robert Louis Stevenson as

> Billows and breeze,
> Mountains and seas,
> Islands of rain and sun.

There were hundreds of islands. I had no choice but to visit some of them.

Maps indicated that the area I needed to explore was twenty-four miles long and a minimum of five miles wide. I was disturbed at the thought of making my way alone among those distant tropical islands. Then I got word that the *Saturday Evening Post* had purchased the rights to publish five parts of the book. The magazine retained Elliot Erwitt of Magnum Photos to accompany me on my trip. He would fly from Paris to Los Angeles to join me. I soon found that he was a marvelous traveling companion and the finest photographer I ever knew.

My most pressing problem was how we were going to get around to those islands of rain and sun. As a last resort before leaving Washington, I turned to the British embassy and to the Seventh-Day Adventists, whose headquarters is in suburban Silver Spring, Maryland. The British had once exercised a protectorate in the Solomons and still had at least some maritime offices there. The person I talked to at the embassy said he would see what could be done to get a boat for me. The Adventists had missionaries on the island of New Georgia, which was the hub of the area I wanted to reach. I told the people in Silver Spring that Erwitt and I were leaving at once for Australia, where I would interview the coastwatcher, Reg Evans. They informed me that we could then take a Quantas Airlines flight to Lae, New Guinea. After a wait, we could catch a plane bound for Guadalcanal by way of New Georgia. That would solve a big problem. The Adventists I talked to promised to notify the missionaries that we were coming and to request that they be helpful to us in any way they could. The help we would receive would be a great deal more than I could have imagined.

When I arrived in Los Angeles, I checked in for the night at the Beverly Hilton. The desk clerk handed me a note to call Olive Montel, the secretary of the *Herald Tribune* bureau in Washington.

"The British embassy called," she told me. "They said they could bring up a boat from Guadalcanal and have it for you at New Georgia the day you got there. I have to let them know right away."

I must have hollered, "Yes!" Then her voice fell. I detected a trace of shock.

"They will want $700 rent," she said.

"Olive," I replied, "if I had to, I'd pay $7,000."

As a means of providing some forewarning about Japanese warships or planes headed toward Australia, coastwatchers were stationed alone during the war in hideaways on islands—Kolombangara in the case of Evans—to inform military authorities in Sydney by radio of enemy movements. Day and night, exasperated Japanese soldiers hunted the coastwatchers with dogs, and they tortured them to death if they found them. Then an officer in the wartime Australian navy, Evans was a professional man, bright, articulate, charming, and, of course, thoroughly familiar with the rescue of the Americans in 1943. He called my attention to the importance of the several young natives who assisted him and who knew the area thoroughly and indeed discovered the whereabouts of Kennedy and his men after the crash. It was they who, in midday, had Kennedy lie in a canoe, covered him with palm fronds, and, although Japanese fighter planes were in the area, paddled him across Blackett Strait to meet Evans. Together they arranged through radio contacts to have other PT boats pick up all the *PT 109* crew.

When I saw him in a suburb of Sydney, Evans had copies of all the radio messages he had sent and received while the crew was shipwrecked. These cleared up the confusion in the men's memories as to the sequence of certain events.

When our plane from Lae descended to the runway on New Georgia, all my concerns about the feasibility and dangers of pursuing Kennedy's course evaporated. "Elliot," I called to my new colleague, "do you see what I see?" From my window, I looked down on the *Kingfisher*, a trim, good-sized yacht waiting at a small dock. In a scene resembling an ad in the *New Yorker*, two or three natives were carrying cartons of Schweppes up the gangplank on their shoulders. (There was no alcohol around, however.)

Standing in line waiting to give us a formal welcome was a group of missionaries. With them were seven middle-aged natives. In their youth eighteen years before they had been Evans's scouts and had helped rescue the stranded American sailors.

Meeting the former scouts was a stroke of luck comparable to obtaining a boat. For a week, they came with us on our voyages and reenacted, chronologically, the movements of Kennedy and his men. No one else could have done this. Unfortunately, they did not know the names of the islands. In such an exotic setting, I did not want to refer to the islands as Island No. 1, Island No. 2, and Island No. 3. When I explained this to the one native who spoke English, Benjamin Kevu, he suggested that the next day we take the boat to the island of Gizo, where there was a British maritime office that had a room full of maps. We did, and we learned that the islands, in order of their occupancy by the Americans, were Plum Pudding, the shape which it resembled, Olasana, and Naru.

The *Kingfisher* had bunk rooms for Erwitt and for me. The captain was Dick Harper, a competent and very cooperative man. A good cook was on the job, ending my worries since before leaving Washington about how I was going to get meals in the Solomon Islands. There was a spaciousness about the craft that was not obliterated by the presence of the seven natives, who slept on the deck. The boat was not a yacht. It was called a copra scow, a term theretofore unknown to me. Copra was one thing; calling it a scow was outrageous. Copra is dried coconut meat from which coconut oil is extracted and used in making cosmetics. Companies like Lever Brothers maintained coconut plantations throughout the Solomons. The "scow" would make the rounds to collect massive piles of copra, which were deposited in the large but inconspicuous holds for shipment to the next processing stage.

From Gizo we went to Plum Pudding Island. When I stepped onto the small beach, it seemed incredible that the man who was now president had once hidden in its heavy shrubbery with his crew to avoid discovery by Japanese scouts. For a souvenir for the president, I took a stick of coral from adjacent reefs. When I saw him in the White House months afterward, he seemed especially delighted with it. I remember his walking along the corridor between the White House proper and the Oval Office, slapping the stick of coral against his thigh. It would have been hard for me to imagine that that piece of coral, shortened and bejeweled, would, some thirty-five years later, bring his widow's estate $68,500 at auction.

While I was still in the Pacific someone, possibly Reg Evans, mentioned to me an event that I found hard to believe. The essence of it was that in the fall of 1943, weeks after the *Amagiri* incident, Kennedy, while in command of another PT boat, had been dangerously involved in rescuing U.S. Marines from death at the hands of Japanese ground forces on nearby Choiseul Island. I had Harper take us to the deserted island, a long strip of sand, swamps, and palm trees. When Erwitt and I went ashore, we found, half buried in sand, a human skull and nearby a battered helmet. Apparently, they supported the report of a battle eighteen years before.

Meanwhile, we were scheduled to take off from New Georgia on a flight to Japan via Lae and Hong Kong. In Tokyo, I interviewed the pleasant Kohei Hanami, former captain of the *Amagiri*, and some of his crew to verify information I had gathered on the collision with *PT 109*. As for Choiseul Island, I had to research the facts in Washington. There had never been occasion for me to speak to President Kennedy about a second PT boat. The matter was not referred to in John Hersey's article. I had never seen anything about it in print. Up to that point, none of the *PT 109* crew had ever alluded to it, nor had any of the president's friends with whom I discussed his career. Once I dug into it, however, the story was there, every bit as dramatic as *PT 109*.

According to navy custom, an officer who has been shipwrecked may return home. Although Kennedy had recently received the Navy and Marine Corps Medal for gallantry in the rescue of his crew, he felt that he had not accomplished enough in the South Pacific to warrant going home. If he could get another boat, he would take it. As it happened, *PT 59* was being refitted as a gunboat, a more powerfully armed craft, to be used against enemy supply barges. Asked if he would like to command it, he said he would and signed, among others, Maguire, Mauer, Kowal, Drewitch, and Drawdy from his old crew. *PT 59* was ready for combat on October 7, 1943. Kennedy headed for his new base in Lambu Lambu Cove on Vella Lavella Island, which looked across New Georgia Sound, called The Slot by the navy, toward Choiseul Island. The island was a main base for Japanese barges.

On October 17, the Second United States Marine Parachute Battalion invaded Choiseul by sea. In heavy fighting with Japanese ground troops, eighty-seven marines were isolated with their backs to the sound. To avert disaster, they would have to be rescued by sea, and that immediately brought the PT boats into the picture. Lieutenant Arthur Berndtson, the base commander, hurried down to the docks in the cove, where he met Kennedy, who was in shorts, a khaki shirt, and an army fatigue cap, watching the men doing chores aboard *PT 59*. Berndtson told Kennedy the frightening news. In the situation, there was no time for delay. The besieged marines were sixty-five miles away.

"How much gas have you aboard?" Berndtson inquired.

"What have you got now, Drawdy?" Kennedy called over. Back came the answer:

"Seven hundred gallons." Capacity was twenty-two hundred gallons. Seven hundred gallons would get *PT 59* to Choiseul Island.

"We could get *over*," Kennedy agreed, but seven hundred gallons was not enough for a round trip, particularly if the boat was jammed with marines. A companion boat in the cove was fully loaded with fuel. Berndtson's strategy was for the two boats to go together. When Kennedy's boat ran out of fuel, the other boat would tow it back to the base. Kennedy lost no time in taking off. Another difficult problem he faced was that the information Berndtson had received did not make clear where a guide boat would be waiting to lead Kennedy to where the marines were fighting for their lives. All Kennedy had was a compass bearing on Choiseul at which a landing craft would join him and give him directions.

The incident reminded me of an infantry night patrol that had lost all expectation of finding what it had been ordered to find and then suddenly bumped into it. All of a sudden, out of the dark at Choiseul Island, were heard voices of embattled marines shouting, "Here's a PT boat!" Kennedy ordered his gunners to fire over the marines' heads to restrain the Japanese attack. In the fighting ashore, Corporal Edward J. Schnell of Wilmette, Illinois, fell with a grievous wound to his chest.

"Doc, don't leave me," he pleaded to Navy Lieutenant John S. Stevens, a medical officer.

"I'm not going to leave you," Stevens replied.

As Kennedy brought his boat close to shore, Stevens told him, "I've got a man in bad shape here."

"We'll find a place for him," Kennedy replied. Amid the scrambling aboard of marines, Schnell was placed in Kennedy's bunk.

"Am I all right, doc?" asked Schnell, who had been recommended to the marine corps by the Wilmette postmaster as a young man who would "serve his country well and with honor."

"Don't worry about it," Stevens said. "You're going to be all right."

At 1 A.M., when Kennedy was on deck, Schnell died in the bunk.

When I was working on the book in 1961, this was the very information I sought. With the help of a medical directory, I found Dr. Stevens's telephone number in Bridgeport, Connecticut. When his secretary got him on the phone for me, he was curious as to why I was working on a book of this sort.

"Do you know who the skipper of that PT boat was?" I asked.

"No," he replied.

"It was President Kennedy," I told him.

"You're pulling my leg," he said.

"Oh, no I'm not," I assured him.

In his weekday book review in the *New York Herald Tribune*, Maurice Dolbier wrote that my book, which ended with the fighting on Choiseul Island, was exciting. But, he continued, "In view of Lieutenant Kennedy's present office, it has added importance as a revelation of the character of the man who now leads the democracies through the dangerous straits of world politics."

The most critical moment for Kennedy was finding, in the dark, the companion boat with enough gasoline to get both skippers back to their base. If *PT 59* could not get a towline from the other boat, Kennedy and his men would drift helplessly to the Choiseul Island shore, where Japanese troops were waiting. Fortunately, the mission ended as planned.

When I finally returned to Washington from Tokyo in July 1961, I found that the *Saturday Evening Post* had decided to combine the final two parts of the book and run them in the Thanksgiving issue. For some technical reason, they would have to have the entire manuscript on the day after Labor Day, which put me in a squeeze. My vacation at the *Herald Tribune* was ended. I had to get up at six every morning and write from 6:30 to 10:00 A.M., when I would leave for the office. The more I wrote, the more I was convinced that President Kennedy should read the manuscript. This was the opposite of my determination that President Eisenhower should not see my book about him before it was published. That was a political book about a president in office who might well feel pressures to request changes in the book that would put him and the Republicans in a different light. The Kennedy book was about a man's experiences in war. He was there; I was not. If I had made any mistakes in reporting eighteen years after the event, he would be in a position to correct me.

As the manuscript lengthened and the summer wore on, Kennedy did not find the time to read the pages. Finally, his press secretary, Salinger, told me that the president was going to the family compound on Cape Cod for a four-day rest. "If we can ever get him to read it," he said, "it will be there." I gave Salinger seventy-five pages to show Kennedy and waited until the following Tuesday for Kennedy to return. Still not a word. Then around 6:15 my phone range in the office. A Secret Service man was calling from Hyannisport, Massachusetts. "Mr. Donovan," he said, "Ambassador Kennedy would like to speak to you." Ambassador Kennedy? What the hell?

"Bob!" came a pained voice. I knew Joseph P. Kennedy through my sister, who had been one of his secretaries in New York for a few years. "Bob," he bewailed. "This is the worst book I have ever read! It's about my own son, and I'm bored to death with it." These words were the very first reaction I heard about the manuscript from anybody.*

"What," he asked, "have you got all these islands in here for?"

"Where," I replied, "do you think the war was ———"

"And what have you got all these Japs in here for?" he demanded.

"Who do you think we were ———"

Again he cut me off. "Why don't you write like Hersey?" Kennedy asked. "He's a good writer."

"Teddy didn't like it either," he added. Then, in a revealing summation, he told me, "Jackie didn't either, but never mind what Jackie thinks." As I was to learn, the former ambassador was wrong on both of these points.

"But that business about *PT 59*," he ruminated, "will be duck soup for the movies."

"I don't give a damn about the movies," I retorted. "I'm interested in writing a good book, and ———"

"Oh," he interjected, "you don't give a damn about the movies? Everyone in the country has money, but the newspaper people, and you don't give a damn about the movies."

To be sure, there was a movie. What I know about its origin is this: Sometime in May 1961, the *New York Times* carried an item from McGraw-Hill Books announcing that it would publish a book by me about Kennedy's wartime adventures in the South Pacific. About a week later, the UP news wire carried a paragraph from Hollywood to the effect that Warner Brothers would, for the first time, make a movie—*PT 109*—about a president in office. McGraw-Hill wrote to Warner Brothers, stating that since it had already announced the Kennedy book, Warner Brothers must base its picture on my work. Hollywood was scornful. What was to keep Warner Brothers from writing its own script? That was the end of the matter, I suspected. Some weeks later, Salinger to my surprise told me in his office that Joseph Kennedy and Jack Warner had agreed to a contract for a movie based on my book. Salinger said that each member of the *PT 109* crew would receive $2,500. On that I would have insisted, as did the president. My share would be $122,000. The terms were subsequently

---

* Ultimately, JFK read the galley proofs. He corrected some dates in his schedule before going overseas. No change was made in my accounts of the actions at sea in which he was involved. Not one of these accounts had come from him. They came from his crew, the natives who rescued them, the Australian coast watcher, and a variety of naval officers.

reported in public, though not the royalties on the hardcover and paperback editions of the book.

Obviously, the president did not object to a movie about himself, but he wanted his father, once a Hollywood mogul, to make sure the deal would not wind up in a mess of some kind. The president also wanted the movie to be based on my book. "The president had enjoyed the book," Salinger wrote in his memoir. "He particularly had been appreciative of the great amount of research done by Donovan, including a trip . . . to the South Pacific where he had found the natives who had rescued Kennedy and his crew, as well as the Australian coastwatcher who had played a key role in the affair."

Work on the movie went forward. The filming was done in the Florida Keys. Late in the fall, the executive producer, Bryan Foy, called to ask me to meet him in Miami to discuss some problems. Bryan Foy was the oldest of the "Seven Little Foys" in the old-time vaudeville act Eddie Foy and the Seven Little Foys. When I joined him, he reminded me that the movie contract would not be consummated until the president approved the actor who would play the role of Lieutenant Kennedy. Foy asked me to talk to the president to get things moving. Kennedy was at Palm Beach. When I arrived the next afternoon, he was out on a yacht until four o'clock. I knew where the dock was, so I rented a bicycle and rode up along a public path. The Secret Service let me wait by the dock. The president landed in good spirits and came up to me and asked, "How's the book going?" "Oh, brother!" I said. "You deserve it," he replied. I told him why I was there and asked him if he had made up his mind on who should play the part of Lieutenant Kennedy. As he often did when he was reaching for an answer, he tapped his right thumbnail against his front teeth.

After a pause, he said, "Jackie would like to see Warren Beatty play the part."

Shortly afterward, I called Foy in Miami, thinking he would be relieved at how fast I had obtained an answer. I did not sense that he was relieved at all, but I had done my part. Four days later, I received another call from him, this time from Los Angeles. He said he was flying to Washington that same day to see me. I reminded him that his arrival would be well into the evening in the East and asked if he would take a cab to my house in Chevy Chase.

When he arrived, my two younger children were hanging over the railing upstairs, curious at the prospect of seeing a high-powered movie director. They were not disappointed. Bryan Foy came through the front door gesticulating like the actor who had played him in a Bob Hope movie on the Foys. In the living room he was hardly quieter, but it was clear that his subject was Warren Beatty. I made no effort to respond, for while I thought Beatty was a good actor, I did not know anything about him personally. Foy pointed to the library.

"You see that big archway there?" he asked.

"Oh, yes," I replied.

"Well, you couldn't get Beatty through it."

"Why not?"

"Because his head's too big."

Foy tried to explain. "The only way Beatty will play Kennedy," he said, "is if Kennedy is a pacifist and won't go to the South Pacific."

That was not quite how I had visualized the movie.

"Beatty turned out to be an intelligent, sensitive young man," Salinger wrote. "He told me there was nothing in the world he would rather do than play President Kennedy, whom he admired, but he saw no future in the picture in the hands of Bryan Foy."

"With Beatty's decision, we were faced with the problem of what to do about the picture," Salinger related. "Jack Warner had put a lot of money into the effort and Donovan had worked hard to produce the book. The president felt that to call a halt to the project would be unfair to both of them." To settle the question of the leading actor, Warner sent to the White House some film clips of various actors. In the end, Kennedy and Salinger chose Cliff Robertson. He lacked Kennedy's sharpness, but on the whole he played his part well. Unfortunately, the movie was second-rate. With the coming of television, however, it has been shown in late-night reruns for years and has helped to preserve the heroic image of John F. Kennedy.

In 1961, my wife and I took our three children to New York for the Thanksgiving weekend. The telephone was ringing as we walked into our suite at the Barbizon Plaza. I grabbed it, and it was President Kennedy calling. He was elated by the success of the book and was very gracious about my work.

"What did your father think of it?" I inquired.

"Here, ask him," the president said, handing over the phone.

"Great book!" the former ambassador exclaimed. "See, Bob, you did just what I told you to do about pace. That brought it off."

I can vouch that the word *pace* never passed between us during our earlier conversation. Concluding the current one, I belatedly expressed my thanks to Mr. Kennedy for persuading Jack Warner to make a movie about *PT 109*.

A few months earlier, the president wrote me:

> The White House
> September 20, 1961
>
> Dear Bob:
> I have read this book with great interest. I find it to be a highly accurate account of the events of the war. I have been particularly interested in the many facets of this story that you have developed that I was not in a position to know at the time.
>
> Sincerely,
> John F. Kennedy

When the movie came out in 1962 the Kennedys invited me and my family to attend a showing in the White House. I had never met Mrs. Kennedy and was enchanted by her feathery voice when she asked me, "How's Kay?" She was referring to my sister, Katherine, Joseph Kennedy's former secretary. He had released her for nearly a month to go to Newport to work with Jack and Jackie as the social secretary for their lavish wedding. Afterward, both of them wrote her effusive letters of thanks.

"By all rights," Jackie told her, "you should have marched up to the altar with Jack."

Think of that! The president would have been my brother-in-law. I might have scooped the *New York Times* every day. But Mrs. Kennedy was writing in niceties and added, "but I'm glad you didn't." The other letter to Katherine ended, "You were terrific—many, many, many thanks—Jack."

In the eyes of my younger children that evening at the White House, the one who was terrific was John F. Kennedy Jr.—"John-John." The president invited us to sit on the Truman Balcony with him while we awaited other guests. John-John came along with a box of toys and began heaving them over the high balcony without even attracting his father's attention.

As usual, however, the Secret Service was on the job. Two agents stood on the lawn below to retrieve the toys and bring them back up in an elevator in order that John-John could keep the air filled with projectiles.

If I am not exaggerating, publication of the book in 1961, dealing as it did with the exploits at sea of a glamorous president, aroused some excitement. As an indication of this, I was invited to appear on the *Today Show*, which would be a new experience for me. I went to New York. A makeup expert did something or other to my face. I was escorted into a room with others awaiting their turn. No manager came by to tell me when I would go on or how I should proceed. I knew no one in the place by name. Then I was silently directed into a studio aglow with lights. In the background on my right hung a large map opposite the chair in which I would be seated. The interviewer made a good deal over my appearance and asked me about my own adventures in the Solomons. Then he assured me that viewers would be fascinated to have me indicate on the map exactly where the action involving *PT 109* took place. If there was anything I knew by this time, it was maps of the Blackett Strait area, having worked with the editors at McGraw-Hill on the maps for inclusion in the book.

With a pointer in hand, I confidently approached the map and then stood back. What was this? Where was Ferguson Passage? Where was Naru Island? I could not just stand there and gawk. I could not wreck the show. Running my eye over the bottom of the map, I could see it was upside down. It was too large for me to reach forward and reverse. There was just one thing to do unless I wanted to embarrass my hosts. Up went the pointer. Here was President Kennedy's boat lurking in Blackett Strait. (The pointer almost certainly was aimed at the center of an island.) And there, returning from Vila on a sweep to the south (the pointer doubtless indicated north) came Captain Hanami's *Amagiri*. "Sound General Quarters," shouted Lieutenant Kennedy. And on it went. Heroic. I stepped back, placed the pointer on the desk, and departed to make room for the next guest. I should have asked politely that the map be righted. Over the years, I was on the *Today Show* a few more times. None confronted me with a map, fortunately.

In the fall of 1961, while I was chief of the *Herald Tribune* bureau in Washington, James B. Reston, the wonderful man who was chief of the Washington bureau of the *New York Times*, invited me to lunch at the Metropolitan Club. When we talked, he surprised me by saying that, although he was not in a position to offer me the job of national editor of the *Times*, he needed to know whether, if the job were offered, I would take it. I replied that I would not. I liked my work in Washington. My family and I loved life in our large old house in Chevy Chase, Maryland. For me to match that kind of living in New York, I would have to be paid far more by the *Times* than I could possibly have been worth as national editor. Furthermore, I was no longer in urgent need of a raise because I had just made a lot of money from my book *PT 109*. Ultimately, the kind of work I was already doing had a much deeper appeal to me than being national editor of the country's major newspaper.

18

CHIEF OF THE *LOS ANGELES TIMES* WASHINGTON BUREAU

One of the most unexpected telephone calls I ever received came around ten o'clock on a Sunday night in the spring of 1962 from a man who introduced himself as Frank Haven, managing editor of the *Los Angeles Times*. He said his paper was looking for a new Washington bureau chief who would be involved in the enlargement of the bureau and inquired whether I would be interested. Despite my enthusiasm for the work I was doing on the *Herald Tribune*, I never forthrightly turned down a job offer. Moreover, the *Tribune* was on the brink of financial ruin. I told Haven I would need to know more about what he had in mind before I could reply. He said that Nick B. Williams, the editor of the paper, would be in Washington for the forthcoming annual convention of the American Society of Newspaper Editors and would answer any questions I had.

The *Los Angeles Times* was the largest and most influential newspaper in southern California. I saw it only when I was covering political stories on the West Coast. A far better product than its rivals, it struck me as a good newspaper for Los Angeles and the huge suburbs. Its local, state, and sports coverage was voluminous. On the other hand, it was blatantly biased toward the Republican Party. Most noticeably, it lacked strong national and international coverage. The Washington bureau then had only a couple of reporters and was little noticed.

Until Haven mentioned him, I had never heard of Nick Williams. When we met in Washington during the ASNE convention, I wanted to work for him. I never before, nor since, encountered anyone in newspapers with a greater mixture of good sense, skill, kindness, decency, erudition, wit, and determination to improve. He was such a modest man it was no wonder I had never heard of him. Everything he offered me, from money to his views on the status, the operation, and the immediate enlargement of the Washington bureau, was irresistible. What was most astonishing was his statement that he would authorize a budget for me to hire as many reporters as I reasonably thought would be needed. I had never heard of a case where a newcomer entered an office and went out and hired a number of people without any interference or approval by higher executives. Literally, this was only half the story. I felt a great responsibility to Nick

Williams to get good people. I did not realize how well certain good reporters in Washington were paid. I cannot recall how much my original budget was, but in a telephone conversation I had to confess to Williams that I could not hire as many people with that amount of money as I had supposed. "Double it," he said. What a contrast with the wonderful old *Herald Tribune*! And of course, I had to act quickly to get us a larger, duly impressive-looking office somewhere near the White House, where real estate is very expensive.

Thus began my fifteen years with the *Los Angeles Times*, all of which were, excluding several crazy months, a gratifying experience. A significant cause for that gratification was that I came on board at a time of reform of the paper, as it changed in ways that quickly established it as one of the best in the United States. Indeed the expansion of the Washington bureau was reflective of those changes.

As early as 1957, Norman Chandler, the elegant and very wealthy publisher, transferred Nick Williams from his rounds of news desks to the position of managing editor and then editor. Chandler instructed him "to do what is right" to give readers fair reporting of events. Acting on his own interpretation, Williams responded by hiring new reporters qualified to give the same kind of coverage to Democrats as to Republicans. At the age of thirty-three, Norman Chandler's son, Otis, succeeded his father as publisher and carried his father's change of heart to the practically revolutionary policy of deciding that the *Times* no longer would use its editorial page to endorse political candidates. James E. Bassett, long active in Republican affairs, was replaced as editorial page editor by the youthful Anthony Day, a graduate of Harvard and the Washington bureau chief of the *Philadelphia Evening Bulletin*, whom I recommended to Williams. What most riled our hordes of conservative readers was the selection of the talented Paul Conrad as the crackling liberal cartoonist on the editorial page.

Otis Chandler, a strapping, handsome man, not only carried on his father's reforms but pushed them further. More bureaus were established abroad. More regional bureaus were opened in the United States. James Bellows, the last editor of the *Herald Tribune*, was brought in as editor of the features sections in the back of the newspaper. Chandler and Williams kept their hands off the Washington bureau but were pleased with it as far as we had gone. As he did with all other editorial branches of the paper, Williams was almost urgent in driving home to us his view that television news had ended newspapers as we once knew them. Television news penetrated homes with news and commentary before we could. Hence, we had to change. We had to do more articles like the leaders on the front page of the *Wall Street Journal*. More offbeat stories were required. We had to find subjects that needed not a day's work, but a week's work. I knew with a certain grimness that these stories did not grow on vines. We did come up with one crackerjack report in 1968—a series by David Kraslow and Stuart H. Loory on behind-the-scenes maneuvering for peace in Vietnam. Indeed, Random House bought the rights and published a book based on the series, *The Secret Search for Peace in Vietnam*.

Loory was our White House correspondent whose critical questioning so exasperated Henry Kissinger that, in his diplomatic style, he told Kraslow and me over dinner that "there will have to be a period of coolness between me and Stuart." Kraslow, a former Nieman fellow at Harvard, who worked in the Washington bureau of the *Miami Herald*, was one of the first reporters I hired. He was such a digger that I thought of him as an investigative reporter, but he soon was in effect the working editor of the bureau, leaving me to my own tasks. When I left, he succeeded me as the Washington bureau chief.

At his urging, I hired Jack Nelson of the *Atlanta Constitution*, a Pulitzer Prize winner, whom I did not know then. In doing so, I brought to the *Los Angeles Times* one of the major figures in the paper's modern history. Nelson later became bureau chief. If I increased the bureau from two to, say, fifteen, Nelson took it from fifteen to around forty-five reporters and desk men. When he turned sixty-five in 1996, he remained as a special writer while the bureau passed into the hands of Doyle McManus. I believe it is now the best it has ever been and wish that Nick Williams had lived to see the result of his own bold efforts.

When I took over the bureau in 1963, I spent so much time getting it into action that I had little opportunity to do reporting myself. So, when the White House announced that President Kennedy would make a political trip to Texas, concluding with a motorcade through Dallas and a speech at the Dallas Trade Mart on November 22, I signed up to cover it.

19

"Where Is the President Anyway?"

The drama in the second press bus, in which I rode in the presidential motorcade in Dallas, is unforgettable.

"Why has the motorcade stopped?" a reporter asked as we drew near the Texas School Book Depository, a shabby-looking building.

"I heard a shot," another said.

A voice in the rear contradicted him. "That was a motorcycle backfiring."

At the moment I was talking to a Dallas reporter across the aisle from me. I had made the trip to write about how President Kennedy fared with Texans roughly a year before the 1964 presidential election. The other reporter was telling me about Richard Nixon's strength in the state.

A call came from the front of the bus: "What are all these people running for?"

I was not surprised. Having ridden in so many motorcades, dozens of them in Truman's and Eisenhower's campaigns alone, I knew it was commonplace for crowds, having watched the president pass, to run across the thoroughfare for a second look at him at his next turn.

While we were stopped, the bus doors opened and a number of us stepped out on the grass about a hundred feet before the Texas School Book Depository. Marianne Means, of the Hearst Newspapers, said that a couple had thrown their child on the ground and fallen on top of it for the child's protection.

Among those of us standing outside the bus, a definite apprehensiveness grew. I resisted it. Covering presidents on their travels at home and aboard had exposed me to rumors of dangers, some of them silly. In Palm Springs, California, with President Eisenhower in 1954, I was startled by a rumor that he had been menaced on a walkway in a resort where the presidential party was staying. I hurried outside, but could find no trace of any trouble.

As I climbed back on our bus in Dallas, someone ahead of me called out, "The president's car is not in the motorcade." I looked toward the book depository. The limousine had vanished. "Where is the president anyway?" someone else asked, touching off a wave of talk over what we should do. It was obvious to most that we should hasten on to the Trade Mart, where Kennedy was due to speak at a luncheon. By now, the motorcade had scattered, and the two press buses rolled through some turmoil in front of the book depository. One of our colleagues, Robert MacNeil, then of NBC, was no longer with us. Convinced that the three sounds he and some others had heard were shots, he was in haste to call his office in New York. The only place he could see nearby where he might find a phone was the book depository. He reached the front entrance of the building quickly, just as a slight, balding, woeful-looking man, a $1.25-an-hour laborer in the building, was hurrying down the front steps. MacNeil asked him where he could find a phone, unaware that the man he was talking to was the man whose name soon would be flashed around the world as, in all likelihood, the president's assassin. Lee Harvey Oswald, who mistook MacNeil for a Secret Service agent, said there was a phone inside the building. The two parted.

From the book depository, our bus quickly passed through a triple railroad underpass. We had scarcely emerged from it when a motorcycle sped between us and the curb on our right and drove up the embankment as far as the vehicle could take the rider, whereupon he jumped off, drew a revolver, and ran along the railroad tracks. I had never before in civilian life seen a handgun drawn, and the sight of it made it more difficult for me to believe that nothing serious had happened. The Trade Mart was only a short ride farther. When we pulled into the parking area, every one of us strained to see the presidential limousine. It was not there.

As soon as the bus stopped, we all grabbed our portable typewriters and scrambled into the Trade Mart, startling guests at their tables, awaiting President Kennedy. Just inside the entrance was a sign, "Press Information, Fourth Floor." Not hopeful, but frantic to learn *something*, David S. Broder, then of the *Washington Evening Star*, and I headed for the escalators. During the ride up, we could look back through a maze of steel girders and see the patient luncheon guests. Like everything else in the last ten minutes or so, the sight was surreal.

The "press room" was deserted, but there were telephones. Broder called his paper and told an editor it might be advisable, briefly as least, to delay a forthcoming edition because something serious seemed to have happened. The editor replied that a bulletin was coming in from Dallas saying that three shots had been fired at the Kennedy motorcade. The reporter of the bulletin, Merriman Smith of United Press International, distinctly heard shots. Smith was a "pool man," or "pooler," representing all the rest of us, and rode in an open car close to the president's while we were in a bus twice as far back.

"Where Is the President Anyway?"

In the Trade Mart, Broder and I rushed back downstairs. He veered off to the buses. I saw a policeman down the hall and hurried to him. I told him that I was with the press and wondered if he could tell me where the president was.

"The president," he replied, "has been shot and may be dead."

"Where is he?" asked a news photographer behind me.

"Parkland Hospital."

With two of his colleagues, the photographer bolted for a door. They let me ride with them. In a twinkling, we were in a station wagon and burst out into the two-lane northbound Harry Hines Boulevard. Never have I experienced such wild speed. As we approached the hospital, now visible on our left, a traffic slowdown was developing ahead of us. Without slowing, our driver swerved into the southbound double lanes. Cars in each of these lanes were coming at us. They swerved. We swerved. The shrieking of brakes was unnerving. The upshot of this insanity was that the policemen directing traffic for the hospital grounds supposed we were officials and waved us right into the driveway where the presidential limousine was parked. Crumpled in blood on the open rear seat was the bunch of red roses presented to Jacqueline when she had deplaned from *Air Force One* at Love Field less than an hour before on that twenty-second day of November 1963.

If Jack Kennedy had been found to have a good chance for recovery, surely that information would have been conveyed to us. The probability that he was dead left me desolate. In my writing of his wartime adventures, I had come to like him very much and was attracted to his quality, wit, and charm. He had known of me from my sister, Katherine, a secretary in his father's office in New York, where he sometimes worked on his affairs when he was in the city. Later Katherine wrote to me: "I respected and liked so much John Kennedy. He was studious and serious and as nice as he could be."

In Washington, I began turning up at his office in the Senate to talk to him about his plans for running for president in 1960. I covered much of his subsequent campaigning and then was brought together with him because of *PT 109*. By the time of Dallas, I felt that he and I would always be friends. The assassination was a cruel loss for many people. I was one of them.

The wait outside Parkland Memorial Hospital called for gloom under black clouds. Instead, bright sunshine jarringly illuminated the trees and the ample lawn around the locked hospital. Together, the lawns and sidewalks formed a promenade in which people strolled back and forth, talking to acquaintances or to complete strangers. Here and there persons stood alone trying to control their emotions. On the sidewalk near the parked limousine stood Senator Ralph Yarborough of Texas, weeping. On the grass was someone I knew, Douglas Kiker of the *New York Herald Tribune*, who looked as though he, too, had been crying. When he saw me, he said, "If I had the power to, I'd call in the bombers over this city." Evidently, he was aware of the strains of hatred of Kennedy in Dallas, although the crowds along the route of the motorcade had been friendly. A middle-aged man I did not know approached me.

"How could a thing like this happen?" he asked.

If he had put the question somewhat differently—inquiring, "What kind of man is it who would assassinate our president?"—then, oddly, he had asked the right person. I was the author of the book *The Assassins*, published in 1952 by Harper and Brothers, much of which had first appeared in the *New Yorker*. The subject of the book was the assassinations and attempted assassinations of American presidents.

The origin of the book dated to another beautiful day, that one in Washington on November 1, 1950, thirteen years before Dallas. I was walking along Pennsylvania Avenue on my way to the Blair House, a historic government guest house, where the Trumans were then living during renovation of the White House. Blair House stands catercorner from the White House in the next block to the west. Those of us reporters covering the president were to gather by two o'clock behind Blair House, where a chartered limousine was waiting to take us to Arlington National Cemetery in a small motorcade with the president, who was to dedicate a monument to Sir John Dill, a member of the Combined (American and British) Chiefs of Staff in the Second World War. When I had just passed the Treasury, near the White House, I heard the shrill of sirens from all directions. Shortly, I could see emergency vehicles clustering in front of Blair House, and I broke into a run. Not glimpsing any smoke, I assumed a fire must have been extinguished. Nevertheless, the closer I got to the scene, the more commotion I could see.

Two Puerto Rican nationalists, Oscar Collazo and Griselio Torresola, had just tried in vain to shoot their way up the front steps and through the front door of Blair House to assassinate President Truman. In the firefight, Torresola and Leslie Coffelt, a uniformed guard, were killed. Collazo, a resident of the Bronx, was arrested. In the hot Indian summer weather, Truman was napping in his BVDs in the front bedroom. When the clamor erupted, he scrambled to a front window to see what was happening, but Secret Service men in the streets waved him back, fearful that another assassin might be somewhere in range of killing him.

The attempt on Harry Truman's life was so extraordinary, I began long-range reporting on Collazo. I talked to his wife twice in New York. I interviewed people who had worked with him in a shop in suburban New Rochelle, where he was a metal polisher. U. E. Baughman, then chief of the United States Secret Service, gave me access to the agency's files on Collazo, who was tried, convicted of the murder of Coffelt, and sentenced to die in the electric chair. Truman commuted the death sentence, and eventually Collazo was freed to spend the rest of his life in Puerto Rico. The essential difference between him and most of the other presidential assassins was that he was a fanatic and they were insane. On this particular subject, Richard P. Nathan, director of the Nelson A. Rockefeller Institute of Government, wrote to me that there are a "lot weirdos out there." A study of the kind of men who kill presidents confirms this.

Offspring of a family saturated with insanity, Charles J. Guiteau, who had practiced for the occasion by firing at saplings along the Potomac River, fatally shot President James A. Garfield in the back in the old Baltimore and Potomac Depot in Washington on July 2, 1881. At his trial, Guiteau maintained that while he held the revolver, God pulled the trigger. Guiteau was convicted and sentenced to be hanged. While a black hood was being put over his head on a scaffold, he recited from a poem he had just written:

I wonder what I will see when I get to the Lordy?
I expected to see most splendid things beyond all earthly
conception.

After Leon F. Czolgosz (pronounced Cholgosh) fatally shot President William McKinley at the Temple of Music at the Pan American Exposition in Buffalo on September 6, 1901, he wrote while being held in a police station: "I killed President McKinley because I done my duty. I don't believe one man should have so much service and another man should have none." A year later the *American Journal of Insanity* published a paper by Dr. L. Vernon Briggs, future chairman of the National Committee for Mental Hygiene and secretary of the Massachusetts State Board of Insanity. After a concentrated study of the life of Czolgosz, Briggs found that for some time Czolgosz had been suffering from delusions. One was that he was an anarchist; the other, that he had a duty to assassinate the president. By this time, however, Czolgosz had been electrocuted. Such was the continuing public wrath over his crime that a carboy of sulfuric acid was poured into his coffin after it had been lowered into the grave. Doctors estimated that the disintegration of the corpse would be complete in twelve hours.

With the death of McKinley, Vice President Theodore Roosevelt became president. In 1904, he declined to run for reelection. In 1912, however, he ran as the candidate of the Progressive, or Bull Moose, Party and set out on a lively campaign. In the midst of it, on September 15, 1912, John Nepomuk Schrank, a German-born New York bartender, wrote a message intended for future publication:

> To The People of the United States:
> Sept. 15, 1901—1:30 a.m. in a dream I saw President McKinley sit up in his coffin pointing at a man in a monk's attire, in whom I recognized Theo Roosevelt. The dead president said This is my murderer, avenge my death[.]

For fourteen dollars Schrank bought a .38-caliber Colt pistol. Then, with a personal loan of $350, he set out by ship and train to intercept Roosevelt on his campaign. On October 14, 1912, on the twenty-fourth day of travel, having covered more than two thousand miles and touched eight states, Schrank had his opportunity in Milwaukee and seized it. As Roosevelt waved to a crowd while standing in his parked car before leaving to make a speech, Schrank moved to within six feet of him and shot him in the right breast, an inch below and just to the right of the nipple. Roosevelt staggered back slightly and propped himself against the rear seat. Death might have been instantaneous except for one of the staples of politics. Roosevelt had written a long speech, folded it, and placed the text in the pocket of his coat, along with his metal glasses case. By the time the bullet passed through the case and scores of pages of paper, the injury it inflicted was only superficial.

The crowd made as if to lynch Schrank, but Roosevelt forbade it. A court-appointed sanity commission examined the assassin and reported unanimously that Schrank was "suffering from insane delusions, grandiose in character and of the systematized variety." The commission concluded that "in our opinion he is insane at the present time." The would-be assassin spent the rest of his life in mental institutions.

One is tempted to say that Giuseppe Zangara, a bricklayer who had emigrated from Italy, had a severe case of regicide. In his native land he had been tormented since childhood with stomach aches. He became convinced that they were caused by heavy work when he was young.

"Where Is the President Anyway?"

"The capitalists get to be boss to my father, keep the money from my father, and my father sends me to work, and I have no school, and I have trouble with my stomach," he testified in court later, "and that way I make my idea to kill the president—kill any president, any king."

In Italy in the early twenties, Zangara bought a pistol with which to shoot King Victor Emmanuel III, but the Royal Guards and crowds stood in his way. A couple of years later—he was vague about dates—he immigrated to the United States. He pondered shooting President Calvin Coolidge but never attempted it. He worked for a time as a bricklayer in New Jersey, after which he moved to Miami. His stomach ache followed him. He decided to go to Washington and assassinate President Herbert Hoover. Before leaving Miami, however, he read that President-Elect Franklin D. Roosevelt would visit the city on February 15, 1933. Since the weather was cold in Washington and would intensify Zangara's stomach pain, he decided to shoot Roosevelt in warm weather instead.

"Make no difference," he later testified. "President just the same bunch—all same. No make no difference who get that job. Run by big money. Makes no difference who he is."

Had Zangara succeeded, who can say what dislocation and panic would have swept the United States in the ensuing months. Franklin Roosevelt was due to be inaugurated as the thirty-second president on the following March 4. If he had been assassinated, John Nance Garner of Uvalde, Texas, the elected vice president, presumably would have become president when the country was all but falling apart in the Great Depression.

At a pawnshop Zangara bought a .32-caliber revolver and ten bullets for eight dollars. On the night of February 15, he made his way into a crowd of thousands of persons at an amphitheater on Biscayne Bay. In the semicircular runway, in front of the stands, Roosevelt entered in the back seat of an open car, waving and smiling. In reality, his speech was a chat about his recent fishing in Florida waters. When he finished, he saw a friend, Mayor Anton J. Cermak of Chicago, in the stands and called, "Come down." Just as Cermak reached the car, Zangara jumped up on a vacant seat in the stands and fired five shots at Roosevelt. The bullets missed the president-elect but wounded four other persons, including Cermak, who died of his wound.

Two psychiatrists and, subsequently, a sanity commission probed around the questions of Zangara's mental condition, but both inquiries avoided a finding of whether he was sane or insane. When the case went to trial, he was found guilty of murder. He was electrocuted and buried in an unmarked grave in prison grounds.

Was President Kennedy's assassin another Guiteau? A Czolgosz? A Collazo? A Zangara? Was he an eccentric who, like many citizens of Dallas, despised Kennedy and all he stood for? Was he a brute who had nothing himself but was suddenly in a position to dispatch a man who seemingly had everything? Was he insane to the point that his conduct was meaningless? Fortunately, or so it was said, the supposed assassin, Oswald, would be placed in the hands of authorities qualified to analyze. But Dallas was simply the wrong place. There was never such an examination.

Two days after the assassination, on Sunday, November 24, at about the same hour that a cortege was to bear John Kennedy's body from the White House to the rotunda of the Capitol to lie in state overnight, Oswald was to be moved from police headquarters to the county hall. At police headquarters, NBC had a live camera in the basement with Tom Pettit as the reporter. Presently, there was a stir. Pettit whispered through his microphone circuit, "Let me have it." Fred Rheinstein, his producer, called over the line to New York, "Give it to us now." A jail elevator door opened. Flanked by two detectives, Oswald, an insignificant-looking prisoner, was led down a ramp to an aisle full of reporters and policemen. In the crowd was a scum named Jack Ruby, completely unknown to the millions watching on television. In Dallas, he was known as the boss of two striptease joints. His cultivation of friendship with policemen and detectives evidently enabled him to slip into the basement, concealing a .38-caliber revolver. As Oswald drew nearer to him, Ruby drew his gun and fired. Oswald gasped and clutched his stomach.

"He's been shot! He's been shot! He's been shot!" Pettit exclaimed into the microphone. "Lee Oswald has been shot! There's a man with a gun. There is absolute panic, absolute panic here in the basement of the Dallas police headquarters. Detectives have their guns drawn. Oswald has been shot. There is no question about it. Oswald has been shot. Pandemonium has broken loose in the basement of the Dallas police headquarters."

Police grappled with Ruby. Oswald was rushed to Parkland Hospital. The same doctors who had tried to save Kennedy's life now tried to save Oswald's, but could not. Among the places where Ruby's shot had been seen were rooms in the White House with television sets.

Theodore C. Sorensen, a special counsel to President Kennedy, asked, "When is this going to end?"

One thing was certainly ended—the plan to have experts probe Oswald's mentality for an explanation of why he might have killed the president. Ruby died of cancer. As with Oswald's, his motives remain unknown.

Earlier, in midafternoon in Dallas on the day Kennedy was shot, the boldest of lingering hopes collapsed with a formal announcement at the hospital that the president was dead. Vice President Lyndon Johnson would immediately take the oath of office as president of the United States aboard *Air Force One* and then depart for Washington, as would the press plane.

After calling the managing editor of the *Dallas News* and obtaining his permission to work at a desk in his newsroom that night, paying for my own Western Union wire to Los Angeles, I decided to spend the night in Dallas. It was not a wise decision because it isolated me. What with the advantageous time difference between Washington and Los Angeles, I could have worked from our own bureau at home. I would have had access to wire-service copy, which I did not have at the *Dallas News*. On the plane I would have relaxed, had a drink, listened to the conversation of some very bright reporters around me, and just looked out the window, musing about how I should handle the story. By contrast, I found working in Dallas tense. A factor that led me to do what I did was that I wanted to take a second look at the scene of the assassination, so recently swarming with people and excitement. Now, I discovered, it was totally deserted, as if out of horror and shame.

In the cab ride to the Book Depository and then the *Dallas News*, thoughts kept tumbling through my head like waters over a falls. For no reason I can think of, the notion came to me again and again that sooner or later Nixon would become president after all. When Kennedy defeated him in 1960, it was plausible that the new president would serve eight years in office. Then, the newly elected vice president, Johnson, would have his shot at eight years in the White House. By that time, someone else would have replaced Nixon as the favorite for the Republican nomination. But now Kennedy was gone, and the future looked very different. I was spinning along on hunches, not analysis. But the hunches weren't wrong. In 1968, Nixon was elected president by defeating Hubert H. Humphrey at the polls.

My head was filled with a kaleidoscope of images of Kennedy. After he won the close election in 1960, he went to Palm Beach for a rest. The second day there he invited the reporters covering him to come to the Kennedy compound for a swim and a drink. At one point, I was sitting on the edge of the pool with my legs in the water, while he was standing behind me in gleaming black shoes, dark slacks, and a white shirt. We addressed him at that point as senator, which was his title.

"Senator," I asked him, "assuming you win a second term, which most people seem to think, by the time you leave office, you will still be only in your early fifties. Then what will you do?"

"I've always wanted to be a rich bum," he replied.

As the evening of the fateful day in Dallas wore on while I was writing my story, I noticed the arrival in the newsroom of familiar faces from the *New York Times*. The *Times* had assigned its regional reporters to Dallas to follow up in ensuing days on various aspects of the assassination, with the immediate task of probing the life of Oswald. One of the newcomers telephoned a nearby hotel to get a suite of rooms and ordered one of them for me. When we all sealed ourselves in the suite, we wanted a drink and rang for a bellboy. The "bellboy" turned out to be a tall, elderly black man with close-cropped gray hair. He told us all the liquor stores in the city were closed, and no liquor was on sale in the hotel. We joined in pleading with him to get us a bottle somehow. He said he couldn't. No liquor was available. Someone suggested he could get a bottle by offering a very high price for it.

"That would be against the law," he said in a slow, deep voice. "There have been enough laws broken in Dallas today."

How lively the foreshortened Kennedy years had been. "Ask not what your country can do for you." A pony named Macaroni grazing on the South Lawn of the White House near Ike's old putting green. *Ich bin ein Berliner*. Pablo Casals playing the cello in the East Room. The rousing welcome for the president in Ireland. The Peace Corps. Jacqueline Kennedy's redecorating of the White House and presentation of the rooms on television. John F. Kennedy Jr. crawling under his father's desk in the Oval Office. The president teaching him how to salute. When the time came for John-John to give the salute at his father's funeral, the sight was unbearable for those who witnessed it.

Particularly, I recall the exuberance of the Kennedy clan and its associates at the time of the inauguration. At one point I was talking to the new press secretary, Pierre Salinger, in the doorway to his office. "The Kennedy administration," he told me, "is going to do for sex what the Eisenhower administration did for golf."

20

Travels with Lyndon

A surprise at the Democratic National Convention of 1960 was the victorious John F. Kennedy's choice of Lyndon Baines Johnson of Texas as the party's candidate for vice president. Political experts were quick to conclude that Kennedy's strategy was to have a running mate who would help him carry southern states against the Republican nominee, Richard M. Nixon. Kennedy's vulnerabilities in the South were that he was a liberal and a Catholic.

Johnson sounded out various Democratic leaders on the best tactics for his task. Harry Truman, not surprisingly, urged him to wage a whistle-stop campaign in the South. The result was that on October 13 Johnson departed Union Station aboard the thirteen-car *LBJ Special* on a hell-to-hominy-grits campaign that would carry him through the Old Dominion all the way south to Louisiana. As I climbed aboard, it looked more like an old Barnum and Bailey circus train than the conventional Truman trains. The last car had streaks of yellow painted on it. Passengers, at least on that car, could not view the passing countryside because political slogans and photographs of Johnson were pasted on the outside of the windows. Perhaps the biggest difference between the Truman and Johnson trains was that the *LBJ Special* carried on the roof a loudspeaker set to blare "The Yellow Rose of Texas" whenever the campaigner approached or departed from a station.

The first stop was Culpeper, Virginia. As the train slowed, Johnson entered the last car, which was occupied by the press, and headed for the rear platform, wearing his "Fort Worth hat," which he used for waving to crowds. When he spoke he placed it on a railing.

"Put on 'The Yellow Rose,' Bobby," he called to an assistant when we entered the outskirts of the town. The music brought cheers from the crowd at the station, and Johnson relished it.

"What has Dick Nixon ever done for Culpeper?" he demanded.

"Why, oh why," he continued, "should the great state of Virginia ever vote Republican? This high-talking, high-spending crowd has never done anything for this section. For eight long years [Eisenhower] Republicans have used the South as a golf course." At Culpeper, as at nearly every stop on the eight-state tour, Robert E. Lee, Sam Houston, Thomas Jefferson, and the Alamo were pressed into service for the cause. Slipped in often was a favorable word for Kennedy's religion.

"Jack Kennedy," Johnson said along the way, "came to Texas and drew 175,000 people in Dallas. I'm proud that the days of Al Smith and 1928 are gone and that the Catholic grandson of a poor Irish immigrant can draw 175,000 in Dallas."

The reference, of course, was to Governor Alfred E. Smith of New York, a Catholic, who, as the Democratic nominee for president in 1928, was swamped by the Republican Herbert Hoover. Several issues were at stake in that election, but bigotry was widely considered a factor in the outcome.

Lyndon Johnson was not the only campaigner aboard the *LBJ Special*. The sweet southern accent of Mrs. Lady Bird Johnson also fell on the ears of voters in Virginia, the Carolinas, and Georgia.

"My daddy," she said, "was named Thomas Jefferson Taylor, my granddaddy was named Thomas Jefferson Taylor, and so were lots of my uncles and cousins—that's the kind of Democrats they were back in Texas."

On the tracks at Lynchburg, Virginia, she appealed: "You all, talk to your uncles and cousins and aunts to keep Virginia Democratic."

As the train was pulling out of Greer, South Carolina, Lyndon Johnson stood on the rear platform, waving.

"Good-bye, Greer," he called. Then, "Bobby, turn off that 'Yellow Rose.'" Then, "God bless you, Greer. Vote Democratic."

Johnson kept up a daily attack on Nixon. What we kept hearing from southerners on the train was that in a recent speech in the garment district in New York, the Republican nominee urged the defeat of Kennedy because he had put a southerner on the ticket.

In a rather menacing Texas idiom in Greenville, South Carolina, Johnson told a rally: "Now I don't know whether there's an old Nixon or a new Nixon. I know there is the same Nixon—the same Nixon that had the smear campaign when he ran for Congress against the fine and upright man named Jerry Voorhis. The same Nixon that had the smear campaign against Mrs. Helen Gahagan Douglas when he ran for the Senate. The same Nixon that said that the Democratic Party coddled traitors when it ran in 1952."

Johnson saved his greatest spellbinding for the county fair in Anderson, South Carolina. He practically drove himself and the large audience into tears over the death of Joseph P. Kennedy Jr., John Kennedy's older brother, who was a navy flier based in England in the Second World War. He was sent on a mission over the Belgian coast and was never seen again. Did it make any difference to the officer who dispatched him, asked Johnson, whether Kennedy was a Catholic? Did his qualifications to fly into combat depend on what church he had gone to that morning? No? Then why should religion bar John F. Kennedy from discharging the duties of the presidency? Apparently, the audience was moved. For a variety of factors, Kennedy carried North and South Carolina, as well as Georgia, Louisiana, Texas, and West Virginia. He lost Virginia. Maybe Dick Nixon had done something for Culpeper. Before the *LBJ Special* had run its course, the Democratic nominee for vice president had a personal word for voters in the Carolinas. "My grandfather, George Washington Baines," he told them, "left here in the 1830s and went to Texas as a preacher and baptized General Sam Houston into the Baptist Church."

The next time I traveled with Lyndon Johnson was a few days after John Kennedy and he arrived in Palm Beach following their defeat of Richard Nixon and Henry Cabot Lodge in the 1960 election. Since they planned no work over the weekend, Johnson invited reporters, all of us from Washington, to make a brief visit to his ranch in the Texas hill country. Although it was dark when our plane landed, he piled us into some waiting limousines. Then, we took off at an extraordinary speed along sandy roads. Here and there, our bright lights were reflected in the eyes of deer pausing to look at us and then bounding away. I never knew how fast we were going, but it was not too fast for Johnson, at the wheel of the front car, to swerve off course to show us something or other about a development undertaken by his grandfather, Sam Ealy Johnson Sr. At another point, he said, "Let's go to see Cousin Oriole." In no time we swept up to a small unpainted cottage standing against a backdrop of brush. No one in that unlighted place could have slept through such a racket. Presently, an elderly woman in a bathrobe emerged. After Johnson introduced us as a group, we were off again. The United Press story by Helen Thomas the next day correctly reported that Cousin Oriole appeared barefoot. Johnson was annoyed. "Does your cousin go to bed with her shoes on?" he asked Helen Thomas.

Then, in 1966, I covered President Johnson's Asian trip, on which he undertook to explain to our allies American aims in the Vietnam War. At the time, even Johnson despaired of the outcome. In a hotel in Canberra, Australia, I was awakened early one morning and informed that I would be the pool man that day on the *Air Force One* flight to Sydney, and would be driven to the airport as soon as I could get ready. Once in the plane, I was assigned to an uncomfortable, solitary seat in the front cabin. The president occupied the well-appointed, closed-off rear section and was accompanied by Prime Minister Harold D. Holt of Australia. Of course, I was eager for news, but not that early in the morning. To doze all the way to Sydney would have been fine. At least I dozed until we reached our altitude for the trip, whereupon Bill Moyers, the press secretary, came forward. "The president," he told me, "would like to introduce you to the prime minister."

When I entered their quarters, the president and the prime minister were seated side by side along the starboard wall. Johnson gave me a bellowing introduction. "Mr. Prime Minister," he boomed, "this is Bob Donovan of the big, bad Republican *Los Angeles Times*." What else could I say but, "Good morning, Mr. Prime Minister"? "Come on, sit down," Johnson invited me. With him in the center, Holt on his right, and I on his left, Johnson resumed a monologue he had been delivering to the prime minister when I entered. Then he broke off and said, "Let's have a soft drink." He pushed a button on his desk. Promptly, a crisply attired Filipino steward appeared. "We'll have three rut beers," the president ordered. If he had asked me what I preferred early that morning, it would not have been root beer.

When the steward headed for the pantry, Johnson resumed his monologue. A few hundred words later the steward reappeared, with a worried look and no tray of glasses. "I'm sorry, we have no root beer, Mr. President," he said. "I could bring you some . . ." Johnson interrupted him. "I said, 'We'll have three rut beers.'" The steward stiffened. "Yes sir," he said, and disappeared again.

The scene was painful. If I could have whispered to him, I would have advised the steward to putter around in the pantry until the pilot was prepared to land in Sydney, halting all service aboard. In fact, this time he was gone so long, I guessed that he was indeed attempting to wait out Johnson. Alas, the door was opened and the waiter appeared again, this time empty-handed and struggling to maintain his poise.

"Mr. President," he began, "I could bring you some Coca . . ." Slowly Johnson leaned forward. His eyes narrowed. "I said, 'Bring us three rut beers!'" he commanded.

However the prime minister felt, I was so embarrassed for the steward that I could barely look at him. *Air Force One* was in the grip of a crisis, and I was sure it would cost the taxpayers. As I imagined it, within hours numerous military transport planes would take off from Andrews Air Force Base, near Washington, laded with cases of root beer for every other air base around the globe where Johnson might land.

The day after our visit to Sydney we were in Brisbane, where we were invited to a barbecue that evening on some prosperous citizen's ranch near the city. Johnson showed up in his best duds from the LBJ ranch at Johnson City, Texas. His tan ten-gallon hat was visible to all. He stationed himself near a paddock, and guests moved in and out of his circle. As I recall, I was drifting close to it myself when Johnson, for no apparent reason, shouted my name. Of course, I responded. Johnson let out a yelp. "Donovan is just the man for it," he told our host. The host had brought out a pair of boxing gloves and asked the president if any of his friends would like to indulge in the Australian sport of boxing kangaroos. Once the president of the United States had selected me, there was almost no way out, unless I ran home to tell my mother. Truthfully, I was curious about getting close to one of the little kangaroos I had seen bounding around the ranch. I would not dream of punching one of them. Presumably, the sport must be sparring. Why not? In the 1920s, at a boys' camp on Lake George in the Adirondacks, I did a fair amount of boxing, enough to keep me from being a novice. Certainly, one of those little bounders could not hurt me. So with the gloves on, I approached the paddock.

Considering a match of this stature, the crowd was very small, I thought. My opponent was led to the scene. Little bounder? He look like a *dinosaur*. Standing erect, he was at least as tall as I was—six feet—and belonged in a higher weight class, certainly. When I entered the paddock, no one took notice particularly. But when the big kangaroo hopped in, he was cheered by Lyndon Johnson. Obviously, the animal was well trained, because he confronted me at once, but not in the way I would have expected. He was not a puncher, which might have hurt an opponent, but a pusher. To my surprise, each of his arms was only about twelve inches long. He could not, as far as I could observe, protect his jaw, but neither could his boxing gloves hit my jaw. Since this was supposed to be a boxing match, I tapped his nose a couple of times. He just kept pumping with his glove, against mine, pushing me backward. I had no intention of punching his defenseless face. I rather liked the old boy, who kept pushing *his* nose toward mine in the manner of Lyndon Johnson's famous "treatment" of shoving his nose toward another man's as a way to dominate him.

Finally, the match with the kangaroo had gone on long enough. I tapped my opponent lightly on the cheek, stepped out of the paddock, and declared myself the winner.

21

THE BIG STORY THAT FELL IN MY LAP

On April 10, 1970, I had a most extraordinary experience. A book by Curt Gentry, *J. Edgar Hoover: The Man and His Secrets*, published by Norton, reported rumors of corruption among high executives of the Federal Bureau of Investigation, including Cartha "Deke" DeLoach, generally regarded as the third-highest official under J. Edgar Hoover. Jack Nelson, an outstanding investigative reporter who had joined the *Los Angeles Times* bureau that same year, dug into the charges.

In a routine telephone conversation with Nick Williams, my editor in Los Angeles, I mentioned Nelson's work as a prospect for a major story. "Bob," Williams said, "that's more than I can take right now." What he meant was that the nonpartisan nature he was imposing on the *Times* had brought an outcry, not only from Republicans and conservatives in southern California generally, but also from the upper levels of the Times Mirror Company. Williams knew he could go only so far so fast. At that moment an exposé of J. Edgar Hoover's staff would arouse fresh anger, or so Williams believed. With Nelson's consent, I assured him we would put the story on hold.

By coincidence, DeLoach, whom I did not know personally, had arranged with a mutual friend to have breakfast with me at the friend's house to discuss the Nelson investigation. He knew that as bureau chief, I had a say in what stories went to Los Angeles. When we sat down at the table, he had a handful of documents to set before me in defense against allegations of financial irregularities. Without preparation, I could not assess the documents very well, but it made no difference, since the story had been killed. I did not mention the matter at breakfast. My talk with Williams was personal. When we broke up, DeLoach did not know he was suddenly in the clear as far as the *Los Angeles Times* was concerned.

A few hours passed. When I was sitting at my desk after lunch, the telephone rang. The caller identified himself as "the man you had breakfast with this morning." It was such an unusual introduction that it took me a few seconds to realize that I was talking to DeLoach.

"If you call the Cosmos Club right away," he said, "and ask for Harry Blackmun, you will find that he is President Nixon's choice to fill the vacancy on the Supreme Court."

The Big Story That Fell in My Lap

In astonishment, I called the club, but Blackmun had just checked out.

No doubt I had been tipped off to a very big story—big because Nixon had been staggered by political squalls in failing to get the Senate to approved two of his earlier choices, Clement F. Haynesworth and G. Harold Carswell, both southerners and segregationists. Haynesworth was from South Carolina, the chief judge of the Fourth Circuit Court of Appeals, and was alleged to have adjudicated a case in which he had a financial interest. According to the second volume of Stephen E. Ambrose's biography of Nixon, Carswell, as a candidate for the Georgia legislature in 1948, had said, "Segregation of the races is proper and the only practical and correct way of life.... I have always so believed and I shall always so act."

Harry A. Blackmun was from Minnesota, an Eisenhower appointee to the Federal Circuit Court of Appeals. Who could doubt that the Senate would approve him? It was to be Justice Blackmun who, in 1973, in one of the most controversial rulings in the Supreme Court's history, would write the majority opinion in *Roe v. Wade*, upholding a woman's right to abortion. My beat on his appointment was top news.

Why did DeLoach, who had known me for only a few hours, tip me off? I could not think of any reason other than that he was offering me a swap. From him I would get an important story. From me, he would be assured that the *Los Angeles Times* would not run a story he apparently dreaded. The Nelson story did not appear. Did DeLoach believe afterward that the Blackmun tip was the reason for this rather than Nick Williams's request? Either way, he and I both came out winners.

22

A Roundabout Way to the Good Years

Glancing back, I recall that Nick Williams, the editor of the *Los Angeles Times*, was so pleased with the Washington bureau's coverage of the Kennedy tragedy that he asked Otis Chandler, the publisher, to call me and express the publisher's commendation of our work.

In his early forties, Chandler was the son of perhaps the most influential family in southern California. Although he served as publisher for relatively few years before moving on to pursue other interests, those years were formidable ones for the paper. The number of news bureaus continued to expand at home and abroad. Circulation grew. Profits rose. Politically, the paper became more objective.

Otis Chandler had a California golden-boy look about him. Tall and broad shouldered, he had a glowing complexion and wavy blond hair. If he resembled an Olympic athlete, it was largely because he had been a champion shot-putter at Stanford. As Williams had requested, he telephoned me to commend me and the rest of the staff at the bureau for our coverage of Dallas and its aftermath. He added that he was coming to Washington soon and invited me to have lunch with him. This was to be the first of several luncheons we would have during his trips to Washington in the next year. Mostly our talks were general rather than professional. But the one I remember vividly was in the fall of 1970, when I took Chandler to lunch at the Federal City Club, and he astonished me by saying that Nick Williams would retire on his sixty-fifth birthday in August 1971, and that he, Chandler, wanted me to become the new editor of one of the nation's greatest newspapers.

I did not say so outright, but my reaction was identical to what it had been when Scotty Reston dangled before me the job of national editor of the *New York Times*. I thanked Chandler, but said that I knew little of southern California, which would be a handicap to the editor of the *Los Angeles Times*. He was not dissuaded. I went on to say that it was important that an editor be knowledgeable about type and makeup. I had not even walked through a composing room since I was a copyboy on the *Buffalo Courier-Express* more than thirty years earlier. I brought up the name of Bill Thomas, the metropolitan editor of the *Los Angeles Times*. As I read the paper in Washington every day, my previous experience on the *New York Herald Tribune* led me to scan the handling of local news in the *Los Angeles Times*. My opinion was that a very good editor must have run that department. Why not promote him, I asked Chandler. He replied that Bill Thomas was still young, that he needed more experience, and that doubtless he would be editor of the paper some day. One thing this told me was that it was contemplated that for several years or so I would be editor in the Nick Williams tradition, until the Chandlers decided on an editor for the long term. At least I wouldn't be expected to undertake a major revision of the *Los Angeles Times*, something for which I had no experience.

Nevertheless, Chandler had made up his mind, and soon I was listed on the *Times* masthead as "Associate Editor." I flew to Los Angeles to talk to Williams. "Nick," I asked him, "do you think I ought to move out here and tackle this job?" He replied, "I hope you will." That settled the matter. I know I was his choice.

With Williams's retirement still a few months away, a number of friends on the paper urged me to come out soon and meet all the executives and familiarize myself with the editor's functions, so that I would feel at home when my turn came. This sounded sensible, and I agreed. It was a mistake. I should have waited until the day Williams left and then assumed his responsibilities. As it was, I stepped into no-man's-land. I had a large gloomy office down the hall from Williams's, but nothing to do in it. While I attended the morning editorial conferences, I left opinions to Williams; he was the editor. I became acquainted with various executives on the business side, but learned little that I had not heard in talks with Chandler and Williams. I rather avoided the editorial department. Theretofore, the managing editor, Frank Haven, had been my superior. Now I was about to become his, and I didn't want to parade around the place. My wife and I were guests at many of the Chandlers' parties.

One morning, when the editorial conference ended, Otis Chandler asked me to join him in his office. When we sat down he said, "Well, the day is almost here." I nodded. "But it is not going to happen," he declared. "This is the worst mistake I ever made." He did not explain. The only concrete statement of his I can remember was that I seemed to be hard of hearing. My lasting regret is that I did not reply, "I can hear you, Otis." He did mention that at the morning conferences I sometimes had to strain to follow the exchanges. Memories of the shooting range in our basement on Auburn Avenue in Buffalo! If being slightly hard of hearing was a sign of aging, that surely would have doomed me with Chandler. But there must have been something more than that behind his decision. In fact, his words were a jolt but not a surprise.

I had been in the business long enough to understand the relationship between publisher and editor. After arriving in Los Angeles, I brought this up with Chandler and said, in effect, it was time we started working on it. He seemed to agree and said a good time to talk would be in April when we were both going to the annual convention of the American Society of Newspaper Editors and would be together on the long flight to Washington. I agreed. What I agreed to, it turned out, was Chandler's settling down in a seat a couple of rows ahead of mine in a half-empty plane and watching movies until we were prepared to land.

The meeting in Chandler's office couldn't have lasted five minutes. He said I could continue working in the editorial department of the paper in Los Angeles or return to the Washington bureau. That decision was the easiest I ever had to make. Chandler went to Wyoming, and I turned to the task of moving back to Washington all the household items as well as the car we had just shipped across the continent. Nick Williams, who apparently knew nothing about what was in store for me, was stunned. He urged me—unnecessarily—not to do anything drastic. In a few hours, I was listening to all the radio and television stations in southern California announcing that the *Los Angeles Times* would have a new editor in the person of Bill Thomas, the one I had urged on Chandler weeks earlier. As I foresaw, the gossip in Washington would be that I was fired as editor of the *Los Angeles Times*. That would have been tough, and some of my old friends still believe it. But I was never editor of the *Los Angeles Times*. How could I have been fired? I simply had the appointment jerked away from me in advance.

What followed for me were the good years. I quickly discovered that when a person is demoted, it is imperative to get him out of the way. Give him a desk somewhere. I still had mine in my old office. No instructions from anyone. Come to the office today or stay home. Bill Thomas did ask me for advice on a new bureau chief. I recommended Jack Nelson, but so did everyone else, and he made a fine one. Above all, I wanted to write, but on my own, and there was no objection to that. I felt I should at least write for the Sunday opinion section. When I had supposed I was about to be editor, I made up my mind that the first thing I would do was install an op-ed-page, a feature that dated at least to the old *New York World*. The *New York Times* had recently done so, and it brightened the inside of the first section compared with ours.

A Roundabout Way to the Good Years

Now that I was back in Washington, I decided to write my own pieces in the op-ed-page style for use anywhere in the paper. I had no regular column. I had no knack for or interest in being a columnist. Among the pieces I did were these:

Sometime after my return to Washington, there was a sharp conflict over national economic policy. I headed for Wall Street to talk to David Rockefeller, whom I had known and liked since I covered City Hall for the *Herald Tribune* and he was, briefly, an assistant to Mayor La Guardia. Now, on Wall Street, he was interested in talking economic policy with me. I took his words in shorthand and made a tight essay of them. The piece had my byline, but the reader saw instantly that the words were Rockefeller's. Soon afterward Nick Williams told me that Otis Chandler liked the piece very much. I even received a letter of praise from Bill Thomas for an article I wrote on the Washington Redskins.

One day I saw an item somewhere about a young woman in Cambridge, Massachusetts, who said that it was impossible for a student to be happy at Harvard in the struggle for high marks. I made an appointment with her and got a lively and interesting piece out of it.

At a dinner party in Washington, I heard a guest say that going to Europe was no fun any more. By chance I had been invited to Paris to attend a conference on, of all things, the motion picture *PT 109*. The film was running in Paris theaters with French dialogue dubbed in. After that I went to London to interview the editor of *Punch*, a renowned humor periodical. I can't remember his name. After telling him what I had heard at the dinner in Washington, I inquired about the current state of humor in Europe. In reply he became so exuberant that he took out a bottle of champagne. When he pulled the cork, the spray saturated my notes. He asked me if I knew Russell Baker, whose wit he admired. Of course I knew Russell Baker, a reporter on the *New York Times* and the narrator of films shown on *Masterpiece Theatre* on the Public Broadcasting System. The *Punch* editor said that he was going to Washington soon and would like to meet him. After his arrival my wife and I took the editor of *Punch* and his wife and Russell Baker and his wife to dinner at the old Provencal Restaurant on Nineteenth Street. No one tried to be funny. It was a delightful evening.

23

What Next?

Not long after that dinner, something happened to me that never could have occurred if I had settled in as editor of the *Los Angeles Times*. A call came from Evan W. Thomas Sr., an editor of W. W. Norton, a New York publisher, who was to become a wonderful friend. The purpose of his call was to thank me for helping a young writer, Tim Smith, straighten out a manuscript Norton wanted to publish and did.

In our conversation, Evan Thomas said that the editors at Norton believed it was time to undertake a history of the Truman presidency. Mr. Truman had left office in 1953 and died in 1972. Evan Thomas, son of the American Socialist leader Norman Thomas, told me that he and his associates recalled that I had covered the Truman administration for the *New York Herald Tribune* and were aware that I had since published two successful books on other subjects. Nevertheless, the thought of writing a Truman book at that point left me cool. I told Evan Thomas that I could not think of anything new to write on the subject. The idea lapsed.

It did not immediately occur to either of us that, with the passage of time, Truman's papers as well as foreign policy documents of that period were becoming open. Evan Thomas kept after me. Yielding, I agreed to visit the Truman Library at Independence, where archivists surprised me with information about how many papers were already open and how many more soon would be. I acknowledged to Thomas that these would be a rich mine, featuring not only the president's personal papers but also his handwritten notes, his secretary's papers, notes on cabinet meetings, the diaries of some members of his staff, and drafts of speeches he never delivered. These were particularly intriguing for a reporter who had watched the show from the front row but could not peer behind the scenes. Evan Thomas and I initially took it for granted that a Truman book would be a single volume. But as my work progressed, the way the information piled up convinced us that the work would have to be divided into two volumes. These were published as *Conflict and Crisis: The Presidency of Harry S Truman, 1945-1948* and *Tumultuous Years: The Presidency of Harry S Truman, 1949-1953*.

During my first few years in Washington I was assigned to cover the Senate. It was a time when the Marshall Plan, NATO, and other administration foreign policy programs were debated and passed. For me this was an education; I came away with a thorough understanding of them. Then I was assigned to the White House in the years involved in the conflicts, the crises, and the political tumult that surrounded Truman. I followed the president wherever he went, including, of course, his whistle-stop campaign, Wake Island, and his vacations in Key West.

Another very important factor for me was that many of the high officials of the Truman administrations, men like Clark Clifford, George Elsey, former Secretary of the Treasury John Snyder, and nearly a score of others remained in Washington after the president's death. These were men whose friendships I had cultivated during the administration. Out of loyalty to President Truman, they usually shrugged off inquiries I made to them as a reporter. Now that Mr. Truman was gone, they were eager to tell me things I could not learn from them before. In a number of cases, their explanations of why the president did or did not do certain things had an authenticity many other sources could not match. In particular, John Snyder, the closest of all to Mr. Truman, was the ultimate source of information and explanation for me. Whenever I wanted to be on the safe side, he was the one I went to.

With the rapid opening of Truman's papers, I was faced with the prospect of having to shuttle back and forth between Washington and Independence. Over a couple of years, the cost of airfare, taxicabs, and motels would be prohibitive. Moving to Independence for the research period would have been out of the question, if for no other reason than that my wife did not want to leave Washington. Thus, the essential problem before me was finding a fine researcher. He or she had to be especially narrative-minded. Indeed, such is also the style of fine historians. The late Henry Steele Commager, I believe, said that history is news. Truman was a rare figure in modern American history, and the researcher had to be able to select material that would capture him as well as his policies and the events that surged around him. The president's picturesqueness could not be allowed to fade among reams of documents. The search for anecdotes must be pursued along with that for dry facts. Who would do this for me? Suddenly, I could exclaim, "I've got my researcher through the CIA." A gem.

A good friend of mine in suburban Virginia was Roger Fowler, who worked in the administrative side of the Central Intelligence Agency, where he scanned matters like job applications. Knowing what I was looking for, he picked out an application by Lawrence A. Yates, who was studying for a Ph.D. at the University of Kansas, which is in Lawrence, a reasonable drive from Independence. I hired him for the years it took me to finish my task. It is a testament to his ability that Dr. Yates then became the supervising historian at the Combat Studies Institute at Fort Leavenworth, Kansas.

After I was well along in my work on the book, I had the enormous good fortune of receiving a fellowship at the Woodrow Wilson International Center for Scholars in Washington, a superb place to work. The center is the national memorial to President Wilson.

Long afterward, in 1997, I happened to visit the Truman Library. Not surprisingly, I was attracted to shelves displaying books for sale on the Truman era. On display were my two volumes, which had recently been republished in paperback by the University of Missouri Press. Underneath the books was a handwritten notice to customers, stating, as nearly as I can recall: "According to Historians These Volumes Are Now Considered the Standard History of the Truman Presidency." If Harry Truman had seen this, he would have been nonplussed. The accepted history of his extraordinary presidency in the hands of a former *New York Herald Tribune* reporter? What next?

INDEX

Numbers in bold refer to photographs.

Acheson, Dean, 47, 48
Adams, Sherman, 50–54, 55, 56, 60–61, 62
Adenauer, Konrad, 81
Ali Jinnah, Mohammed, 78
Ambrose, Stephen E., 47, 85, 129
American Journal of Insanity, 117
Anderson, Cliff, 107
Anderson, Dillon, 60–61, 63
Andrews, Bert, 70, 72
Appleton, John, 53
Associated Press, 45, 70, 71
Atatürk, Kemal, 77
Atlanta Constitution, 112
Attlee, Clement R., 44

Baines, George Washington, 125
Baker, Russ, 78, 80–81, 133
Barkley, Alben W., 38
Bassett, James E., 111
Baughman, U. E., 117
Beatty, Warren, 106–7
Bellows, James G., 72, 111
Benedict XV, Pope, 76
Berndtson, Arthur, 102–3
Blackmun, Harry, 128–29
Bradley, Omar N., 47
Broder, David S., 114–15
Buffalo Courier-Express, x, 2–7, 26, 30, 130; demise of, 7
Burke, Arleigh, 95–96
Burton, Theodore Elijah, 84

Carswell, G. Harold, 129
Casals, Pablo, 122
Castro, Fidel, 73, 97
Celler, Emanuel, 63
Cermak, Anton J., 119
Chandler, Norman, 111
Chandler, Otis, 111, 130–33
Chicago Daily News, 80
Chicago Tribune, 35, 66
Christian Science Monitor, 64, 70
Churchill, Winston, 35
Cleveland, Grover, 1

Clevenger, Cliff, 35
Clifford, Clark M., 37, 135
Clinton, Bill, 40, **91**
Cobb, Joe, 19
Coffelt, Leslie, 116–17
Coffin, Tris, 31–32
Collazo, Oscar, 116–17
Collier's, 51, 52; demise of, 69
Commager, Henry Steele, 135
Conrad, Paul, 111
Coolidge, Calvin, 83, 119
Coolidge, Grace, 83
Cornish, George, 53, 57, 70
Cousins, Robert, 83
Coxey, Jacob S., 83
Cutler, Robert, 56–57
Czolgosz, Leon F., 117

Daily Worker, 53
Dallas News, 121
Dallinger, Fredrick W., 85
Dawson, William L., 62
Day, Anthony, 111
Dearing, Paul W., 26–27
De Gaulle, Charles, 27, 81
DeLoach, Cartha "Deke," 128–29
Denson, John, 71
Dewey, Thomas E., 34, 84; 1944 campaign, 30; 1948 campaign, 38, 39
Dill, Sir John, 116
Dolbier, Maurice, 104
Donovan, Katharine "Kay" (sister), 21, 104, 108, 115
Donovan, Martha (wife), 12, 21, 26–27, 46, 107, 133, 135
Donovan, Michael J. (father), 1
Donovan, Patricia (daughter), 26–27
Donovan children, 107
Douglas, Helen Gahagan, 124
Drawdy (*PT 109* crew), 98, 102
Drewitch (*PT 109* crew), 98, 102
Drummond, Geoffrey, 33
Drummond, Roscoe, 33, 51, 70
Dulles, Allen W., 56
Dulles, John Foster, 55–56

Eisenhower, Dwight D., ix, 47, 68, 73, 85, 95, 97, 113, 122, 129; *Air Force One* trip, 75–82; book about, 50–54, 59–65, 104; 1952 campaign, 28, 38; helicopter, 65–66; 1952 inauguration, 48; suits, 32; World War II, 2, 14, 24, 27
Elsey, George M., 37, 43, 135
Engelking, L. L. "Engel," 7
Erwitt, Elliot, 99–101
Evans, Reg, 99–100
Evans, Rowland, Jr., 71

Fillmore, Millard, 1
Folliard, Eddie, 38
Ford, Gerald, **89**
Fowler, Roger, 135
Foy, Brian, 106–7
Franco, Francisco, 81
Frost, Robert, 68

Garfield, James A., 117
Garner, John Nance, 119
Gentry, Curt, 128
Gerow, Leonard T., 24
Glaser, Vera R., 53
Goodpaster, Andrew J., 60–61, 80
Griggs, L. Vernon, 117
Gronchi, Giovanni, 75
Guiteau, Charles J., 117

Hagerty, James C. "Jim," 66–67, 79
Hall, William, 74
Halleck, Charles A., 83
Hanami, Kohei, 98, 102, 109
Harper, Dick, 101
Harris (*PT 109* crew), 98
Haven, Frank, 110, 131
Haynesworth, Clement F., 129
Hearst Newspapers, 113
Hersey, John, 95–96, 102, 105
Higgins, Marguerite "Maggie," 71, 72–74
Hirschfelder, Chester, 24
Hitler, Adolf, 2, 5, 16, 17, 20–21, 24, 25, 47
Holmes, Jack, 23
Holt, Harold D., 125–26
Hoover, Herbert, 85, 119, 124
Hoover, J. Edgar, 128

Hope, Bob, 106
Hopkins, Harry, 50
Houston, Sam, 123, 125
Hughes, Charles Evans, 83
Humphrey, Hubert H., 121

Il Momento, 44
International News Service, 44
Irwin, Don, 71

Jefferson, Thomas, 123
John XXIII, Pope, 76
Johnson, Lyndon B., ix, **88**, 121, 125–27; 1960 campaign, 123–25
Johnson, Lady Bird, 124
Johnson, Sam Ealy, Sr., 125
Johnston (*PT 109* crew), 98
Journal of Commerce, 71

Kennedy, Edward, 105
Kennedy, Jacqueline, 105, 106, 108, 122
Kennedy, John F., ix, 73, 74, **86**, **87**, **88**, 92, 93, 112; 1960 campaign, 123–25; assassination of, x, 113–16, 120–22, 130; book about *PT 109* and *PT 59*, 95–109
Kennedy, John F. "John-John," Jr., 108, 122
Kennedy, Joseph P., 95–96, 104, 105, 107, 108
Kennedy, Joseph P., Jr., 124
Kennedy, Robert, 73, 82
Kevu, Benjamin, **88**, 101
Khrushchev, Nikita, 74, 95
Kiker, Douglas, 116
King, Theodore Roosevelt, 31
Kirksey, Andrew Jackson (*PT 109* crew), 98
Kissenger, Henry, 112
Klein, Herbert G., 57–58
Kluger, Richard, 63, 71
Kowal (*PT 109* crew), 98, 102
Kraslow, David, 112
Kuhn, Ed, 95–96

La Guardia, Fiorello H., ix, 8–12, 22, 58, 76, 133
Lambert, Tom, 71

Index

Lee, Robert E., 123
Life, 56
Linkins, Carroll "Linc," 36, 45
Lippmann, Walter, 2, 5
Lisagor, Peter, 80
Lodge, Henry Cabot, 125
Loftus, Joseph A., 66
Loory, Stuart H., 112
Los Angeles Times, ix, 82, 91, 126, 128–29, 130–33, 134; becoming Washington bureau chief of, 110–12

MacArthur, Douglas A., 92; meeting with Truman, 41–43
Macmillan, Harold, 81
MacNeil, Robert, 114
Magnum Photos, 99
Maguire (*PT 109* crew), 98, 102
Mamey, Harold (*PT 109* crew), 98
Marshall, George C., 47
Martin, Joseph W., Jr., 51; book about, 83–85
Mauer (*PT 109* crew), 98, 102
Mazo, Earl, 71, 73
McCann, Kevin, 50, 81
McCarthy, Joe, 50, 58, 62; McCarthy era, 52
McClellan, John, 63
McGaffin, William, 66
McKinley, William, 83, 117–18
McLendon, Charles, 5, 6
McLennan, Fred, 2
McMahon, Patrick (*PT 109* crew), 98
McManus, Doyle, 112
McNamera, Robert S., 92
Means, Marianne, 113
Mellen, Calvert K. "Cap," 2
Miami Herald, 112
Minnich, Arthur, 51, 59
Mohamad V of Morocco, 81
Montel, Olive, 99–100
Montgomery, Robert, 59
Morris, Newbold, 32
Moses, Robert, 10
Moyers, Bill, 126
Munroe, Mary, 97
Munroe, Patrick, 97
Murphy, Charles S., 43
Myers, Joe, 2

Nathan, Richard P., 117
NBC, 114, 120
Nehru, Jawaharlal, 80
Nelson, Jack, **91**, 112, 128–29, 132
Newark News, 92
Newsday, 74
Newsweek, 71,
New York Daily News, 44
New Yorker, 7, 52, 63, 95
New York Herald Tribune, ix, 25, 26, 29, 30, 33, 36, 46, 56, 57, 59, 60, 79, 97, 99, 104, 109, 110, 116, 131, 133, 134, 136; Eisenhower's favorite paper, 50; getting hired at, 5–7; killing a story, 92–94; leave from, to work on Eisenhower book, 51–53; New York City Hall beat, 8; Paris edition of, 26, 72; return to, after World War II, 12; Truman's opinion of, 40; Washington bureau, 72–74; as Washington bureau chief of, 70–71
New York Post, 27
New York Times, 5, 62, 66, 70, 80, 105, 108, 122, 130, 132, 133; job offer from, 109
New York Times Book Review, 64
New York World, 132
Nicholson, Henry J., 34, 41–42
Nixon, Pat, 82
Nixon, Richard M., ix, 57–58, 70, 82, **89**, 113, 121; 1960 campaign, 123–25; Supreme Court nominations of, 128–29
Nixon, Robert G., 44–46
Novak, Robert, 71

O'Connor, James, 85
Oswald, Lee Harvey, 114, 120, 122

Pettit, Tom, 120
Philadelphia Evening Bulletin, 111
Punch, 133

Quill, Mike, 53

Rabb, Maxwell, 63
Rappaport, Sam, 14
Reagan, Ronald, **90**

Reardon, Ted, 95
Reid, Ogden "Brownie," 52, 70
Reid family, 5–6, 53, 70
Reston, James B. "Scotty," 109, 130
Reza Pahlavi, Shah Mohammad, 81
Rheinstein, Fred, 120
Robertson, Walter M., 22, 24
Robinson, William E., 59
Rockefeller, David, 133
Rogers, Edith Nourse, 85
Rogers, Warren, Jr., 71, 92–93
Roosevelt, Eleanor, 13
Roosevelt, Franklin D., 2, 29–30, 69, 83, 119; death of, 29; meeting with MacArthur, 41–42; plane used by, 75; World War II, 13, 17
Roosevelt, Theodore, 118
Ross, Charlie, 40, 42, 44, 46
Ross, George "Barney" (*PT 109* crew), **88**, 98
Rovere, Richard H., 63–64
Ruby, Jack, 120

St. Louis Post-Dispatch, 46, 64
Salinger, Pierre, 93, 96–97, 104, 105, 122
Sanford, Terry, 73
Saturday Evening Post, 69, 99, 104
Schnell, Edward J., 103
Schrank, John Nepomuk, 118
Shepley, James, 56
Sirovich, William I., 85
Slevin, Joseph, 71
Smith, Al, 124
Smith, Merriman, 114
Smith, Red, 5
Smith, Tim, 134
Snyder, John W., 48, 135
Sorensen, Theodore C., 120
Sousa, John Philip, 84
Spectator, 70
Stalin, Joseph: death of, 50; Truman's remarks about, 35–37
Starkey (*PT 109* crew), 98
Stars and Stripes, 26, 29
Stephens, Thomas E., 32
Stevens, John S., 103
Stevens, Thaddeus, 35
Stevenson, Adlai E., 51; 1952 campaign, 38

Stevenson, Robert Louis, 99
Stout, Richard, 64
Sylvester, Arthur, 92, 94

Taft, Martha, 34
Taft, Robert A., 35, 84; 1952 campaign, 28; whistle-stop campaigning, 33–34
Taft, William Howard, 33
Taylor, Thomas Jefferson, 124
Thomas, Bill, 130–33
Thomas, Evan W., Sr., 134
Thomas, Helen, 125
Thomas, Norman, 134
Times of India, 44
Today Show, 108
Torresola, Griselio, 116
Toth, Robert C., 71
Truman, Bess, 48
Truman, Harry S., 30–31, 34–35, **90**, 92, 123; 1948 campaign, x, 38–40; and Eisenhower candidacy, 47, 48; attempted assassination of, 116–17; becomes president, 29; book about, ix, 134–36; departure from Washington, 48–49; and Korea, 43–46; meeting with General MacArthur, 41–43; plane used by, 75; whistle-stop campaigning, 33–34
Truman, Margaret, **86, 90**
Twain, Mark, 39

United Press, 45, 114, 125

Victor Emmanuel III, 119
Von Rundstedt, Gerd, 21
Voorhis, Jerry, 124

Wald, Richard C., 72
Wallace, Henry A., 29
Wall Street Journal, 112
Warner, Jack, 105, 107
Warner, James E., 56
Washington Evening Star, 49, 114
Washington Post, 38, 92
Washington Times-Herald, 31
Wayne, "Mad Anthony," 34
Whitehead, Don, 70

Index

Whitman, Ann, 75, 80, 81
Whitney, John Hay "Jock," 33, 93
Wilcox, Grafton, 7
Williams, Nick B., 110–12, 128–29, 130–33
Willkie, Wendell L., 83, 84
Wilson, Woodrow, 76, 83, 136
Wise, David, 70, 74, 92 93
Woodward, Stanley, 5

Yarborough, Ralph, 116
Yates, Lawrence A., 135–36
Yerxa, Fendall, 92–93

Zahir Shah, Mohammed, 79
Zangara, Guiseppe, 118–19
Zinzer (*PT 109* crew), 98

UNIVERSITY LIBRARY
k as s   es yo   ave
ert   st